The BIG
Book of CHINA

Qicheng Wang

A Guided Tour
Through 5,000
Years of History and
Culture

LONG RIVER PRESS

ISBN 978-1-59265-088-0

Published in the United States of America by

Long River Press
360 Swift Avenue, Suite 48
South San Francisco, CA 94080
www.longriverpress.com

Library of Congress Cataloging-in-Publication Data

Wang, Qicheng, 1973-
  The big book of China : a guided tour through 5,000 years of
history and culture / Qicheng Wang.
      p. cm.
  ISBN 978-1-59265-088-0
  1. China--Juvenile literature. I. Title.
  DS706.W325 2010
  951--dc22
                              2009048365

Printed in China

First Edition

* This book uses the metric system of measurements
  because it is the standard used in China today.

The BIG
Book of CHINA

Isn't it great to meet friends from afar!

Hi everyone!
I'm your friend Qi Qi.
In this lovely and very different
illustrated book, you and I are going
on a wonderful journey to a faraway
place ...

It's an ancient Eastern country ...

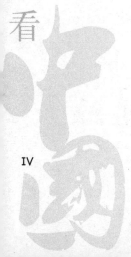

China

Preface

Preface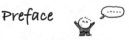

On this beautiful planet where we live, there's a country with a 5,000-year history of civilization. Embracing a vast land of great diversity and beauty in the world's East, this ancient culture has developed at an amazing speed. This country's name is- China.

Through this lovely and very different book, I will be your young guide on a fun tour across China, along its long river of history, unveiling the mysteries of this ancient nation of Asia. During our journey across this land shaped like a rooster, let us take a joy-filled ride to appreciate the incredible beauty of its rivers and mountains, savor the glory and brilliance of its fascinating culture, take a glimpse into the lives of today's Chinese people and discover the secret potions for China's magically flowering economy.

"Isn't it a pleasure to meet friends from afar!" the ancient Chinese sage Confucius conveyed this greeting to the world 2,000 years ago. And today, with the sincerity of all the welcoming Chinese people, I extend to you my warmest invitation.

Welcome to China!

Your Friend,
Qi Qi

Contents

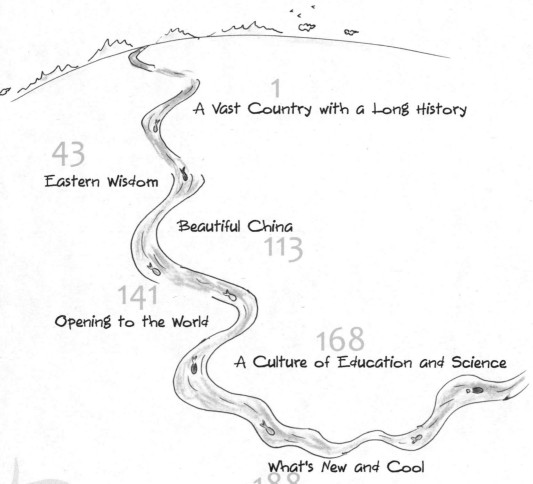

01

A Vast Country with a Long History

China is located in the eastern part of the Asian continent and on the western shores of the Pacific, far off across this ocean on the other side is the United States of America.

Pacific Ocean

China is located in the eastern part of the
Asian continent and on the western shores of
the Pacific Ocean.

Ancient Chinese people believed
that the sky was round and the
earth was square, that China
was in the middle, so they named
the country "Zhongguo," or the
Middle Kingdom.

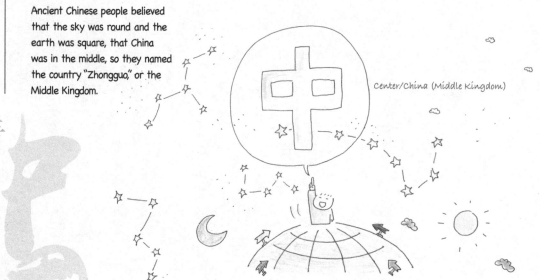

Center/China (Middle Kingdom)

2

Over its 5,000 years of civilization, the Chinese people - comprising 56 ethnic groups - have created an incalculably precious historical legacy.

Vast Territory

The map of China looks like a rooster with its head facing east. The country is about 5,500 km long from north to south and 5,200 km long from east to west.

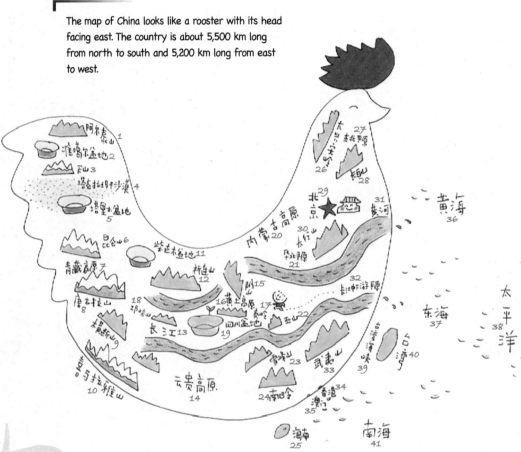

1 Altai Mountains	15 Yinshan Mountains	29 Beijing
2 Junggar Basin	16 Loess Plateau	30 Taihang Mountains
3 Tianshan Mountains	17 Qinling Mountains	31 Yellow River
4 Taklimakan Desert	18 Qionglai Mountains	32 Middle and Lower Yangtze Valley Plains
5 Tarim Basin	19 Sichuan Basin	33 Wuyi Mountains
6 Kunlun Mountains	20 Inner Mongolia Plateau	34 Hong Kong
7 Qinghai-Tibetan Plateau	21 North China Plain	35 Macao
8 Danggula Mountains	22 Mount Wu	36 Yellow Sea
9 Hengduan Mountains	23 Xuefeng Mountains	37 East China Sea
10 The Himalayas	24 Nanling Mountains	38 Pacific Ocean
11 Qaidam Basin	25 Hainan Island	39 Taiwan Straits
12 Qilian Mountains	26 Greater Xing'an Mountains	40 Taiwan Island
13 Yangtze River	27 Northeast Plain	41 South China Sea
14 Yunnan-Guizhou Plateau	28 Changbai Mountains	

The Qinghai-Tibetan Plateau- Roof of the World

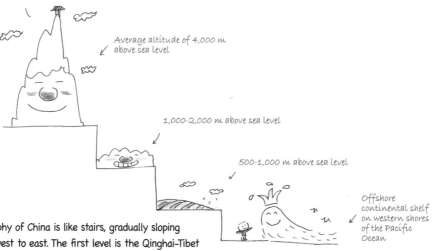

Average altitude of 4,000 m above sea level

1,000-2,000 m above sea level

500-1,000 m above sea level

Offshore continental shelf on western shores of the Pacific Ocean

The topography of China is like stairs, gradually sloping down from west to east. The first level is the Qinghai-Tibet Plateau, averaging more than 4,000 m above sea level; the second level consists of the Inner Mongolia Plateau, the Loess Plateau and the Sichuan Basin, averaging 1,000 m to 2,000 m above sea level; the third level is made up of the Northeast Plain, the North China Plain and the Middle and Lower Yangtze Valley Plains, averaging 500 m to less than 1,000 m above sea level; and the fourth level is the offshore area of continental shelf on the western shores of Pacific Ocean, where the water depths are less than 200 m.

China has a land area of 9.6 million sq km, and is the third largest country in the world, next only to Russia and Canada. China is almost as big as the whole of Europe. About 70% of China's land consists of hills, plateau and hilly terrain, while the rest are basins and plains.

俄罗斯
Russia

加拿大
Canada

960万平方公里
9,600,000 sq. km

欧洲
Europe

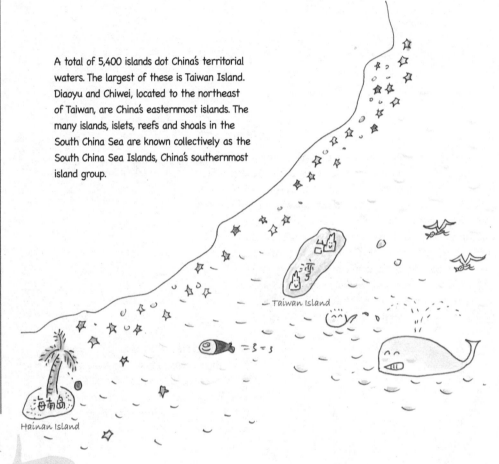

A total of 5,400 islands dot China's territorial waters. The largest of these is Taiwan Island. Diaoyu and Chiwei, located to the northeast of Taiwan, are China's easternmost islands. The many islands, islets, reefs and shoals in the South China Sea are known collectively as the South China Sea Islands, China's southernmost island group.

Taiwan Island

Hainan Island

6

Variety of Climate Types

The climate of China has distinct features of a monsoon climate, characterized by a continental monsoon climate and a variety of climate types. In winter, it is cold and dry with northern winds and low temperatures. There are great differences between the temperatures of northern and southern parts of China, a range which can be more than 50°C.

Beijing, the capital city of China, has a distinctive climate. In spring, flowers blossom; while summer is hot and rainy. Autumn is the best season in Beijing when the climate is cool, and winter is cold and dry.

Spring   Summer   Autumn   Winter

Mohe is the northernmost city in China, and is also the coldest place in winter in the country. The average temperature of Mohe in January is –30.6℃. Summer in Mohe is very short, lasting from mid-July to the end of the month, but daylight is long while nighttime is short in that period, with the longest day lasting 19 hours. Therefore, it is nicknamed the "sleepless city." Mohe is the only city in China where people can see the aurora borealis, or northern lights.

Chongqing, Wuhan and Nanjing are known as the "three furnaces" in China. Every year there are 15 to 35 days when temperatures soar above 35℃ in these cities. But the hottest place in China during summertime is Turpan in Xinjiang. The average temperature of Turpan in July is 33℃, and the temperature once reached as high as 49.6℃.

Hainan Island is on the same latitude as Hawaii in the United States. The coastline of Hainan is 1,528 km long, making it a wonderful tourist resort. The climate on Hainan Island is pleasant all year round. In winter, when cold winds and snow hit northeast China, many people travel south to enjoy themselves on the warm beaches of Hainan Island.

The summers in Tibet are cool and its winters are cold, with temperatures dropping as the altitude rises. Temperatures drop 0.6°C on average with each 100m altitude increase. Areas with altitudes above 4,500 m experience winter weather all year round. The annual average temperature of Lhasa is 7.5°C. The highest temperature in June is 29.4°C, but drops to 0°C–5°C at night. Therefore, Tibetan people have the custom of keeping one arm outside the sleeve during the day, while tightening up clothes at night to keep warm.

Located in northwestern China, Xinjiang is far from the sea and bordered by high mountains. The region has strong sunshine, a dry climate, cold winters and hot summers, sandy winds, and large temperature differences between day and night. One seems to experience summer and winter within one day. Temperature differences are conducive to the accumulation of carbohydrates in fruits, therefore Xinjiang's Hami melons, watermelons, grapes, apricots, peaches and pears are especially sweet and delicious.

Yangtze River, the Longest River in China

The Yangtze River, as China's longest river (the meaning of its Chinese name, Changjiang) and the world's third longest, is the main east-west artery of water transport in the country. With its source in the Qinghai-Tibet Plateau, the Yangtze River flows from northwest to southeast, with a total length of 6,300 km. Its main channel passes through Qinghai, Tibet, Sichuan, Yunnan, Chongqing, Hubei, Hunan, Jiangxi, Anhui, Jiangsu and Shanghai, finally flowing into the Pacific Ocean at Chongming Island.

看

With several thousand tributaries, the Yangtze River valley covers an area of more than 1,800,000 sq km, including nearly 200 cities. The river can be divided into three parts, each part having a different type of scenery: in the river's upper reaches from the source to Yichang, the river flows through precipitous mountain valleys; in the middle reaches from Yichang to Hukou, the Yangtze River feeds many tributaries and lakes; in its lower reaches from Hukou to the estuary, the Yangtze becomes smooth and wide.

The Yangtze River area is a great granary for China, with its grain production accounting for almost half of total national production. The production of rice in the area accounts for 70% of China's total production. Moreover, cotton, wheat, barley, corn and soybean are planted in the area. Major cities such as Shanghai, Nanjing, Wuhan, Chongqing and Chengdu are situated in the Yangtze River area.

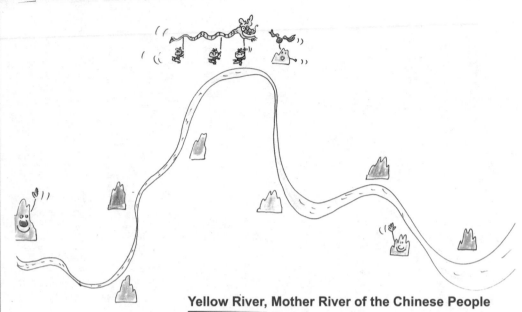

Yellow River, Mother River of the Chinese People

This major river flows 5,464 km through the northern part of China. Looking from the sky, the river resembles a giant Chinese character 几 "ji," or like a flying dragon. The Yellow River (Huanghe) is the second longest river in China. Originating from Qinghai Province, the Yellow River is situated at latitudes approximate to the American states of Virginia, Kansas and Nevada, and countries like Greece and Turkey.

In its upper reaches, the river runs through a large but sparsely populated mountainous area; and in the middle reaches, the river passes through the densely populated Loess Plateau, carrying with it the silt to downstream. In the lower reaches, the river is silted up so the river channel is much higher than the surrounding land, forming an elevated river.
Because its water contains too much silt, the Yellow River has always been the most difficult river to control in China.

China's civilization emerged in the Yellow River basin, so the Chinese people often refer to it as the cradle of Chinese civilization. Since the 21st century BC, there has been over 3,000 years when different dynasties established capitals in the Yellow River region. The "Four Great Inventions" of ancient China, i.e. papermaking technology, printing technology, compass and gunpowder, all took place in the Yellow River region.

Like ancient India and Babylonia, advanced agricultural civilization was cultivated in the major river regions of China. The large amounts of loess in the Yellow River region make it suitable for growing millet and broomcorn millet which do not require much water. The many lakes and rivers in the Yangtze River region means rice is widely planted and the region is lauded as the "land of fish and rice."

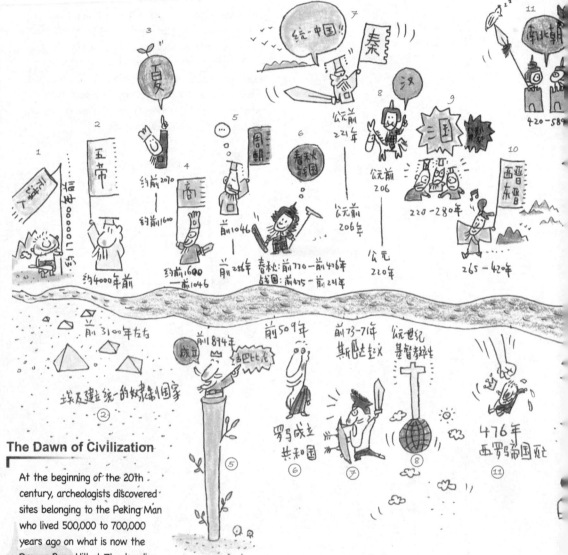

The Dawn of Civilization

At the beginning of the 20th century, archeologists discovered sites belonging to the Peking Man who lived 500,000 to 700,000 years ago on what is now the Dragon Bone Hill at Zhoukoudian in Beijing. They also found sites belonging to the Upper Cave Man from 18,000 years ago. The Upper Cave Man was able to produce multifunctional stone implements. The bone needles found at the site revealed that humans had already ended the period of being unclothed by then.

1 Yuanmou Man c. 1,700,000 years ago
2 Five Emperors c. 4,000 years ago
3 Xia Dynasty c. 2070-1600 BC
4 Shang Dynasty c. 1600-1046 BC
5 Zhou Dynasty 1046-256 BC
6 Spring and Autumn and Warring States Period
Spring and Autumn Period 770-476 BC
Warring States Period 475-221 BC
7 Unification of China
Qin Dynasty 221-206 BC
8 Han Dynasty 206 BC - AD 220
9 Three Kingdoms Period, in split AD 220-280
10 Western Jin and Eastern Jin Dynasties 265-420
11 Southern and Northern Dynasties, in split 420-589
12 Sui Dynasty 581-618
13 Tang Dynasty 618-907
14 Five Dynasties and Ten Kingdoms, in split 907-960
15 Song Dynasty 960-1279
16 Yuan Dynasty 1206-1368
17 Ming Dynasty 1368-1644
18 Qing Dynasty 1616-1911
19 Republic of China 1912-1949
20 People's Republic of China 1949 to present

② c. 3100 BC Unified slave society in Egypt
⑤ 1894 BC Ancient Babylon
⑥ 509 BC Roman Republic
⑦ 73-71 BC Slave Uprising of Spartacus
⑧ 1st Century AD Birth of Christ
⑪ AD 476 Downfall of the Western Roman Empire
⑬ AD 622 Muhammad's Hegira from Mecca to Medina
⑮ AD 962 Holy Roman Empire
⑯ 14th-16th centuries Renaissance in Europe
⑰ 1519-1522 Magellan's Circumnavigation of the Globe
⑱ July 4, 1776 Founding of the United States of America
⑲ 1914-1918 First World War
⑳ 1939-1945 Second World War

From 3,500 BC to 3,100 BC in Egypt, the Pharaohs and hieroglyphic writing appeared. The first documented dynasty in China appeared in 2070 BC, the Xia Dynasty, marking the first kingdom in Chinese history.

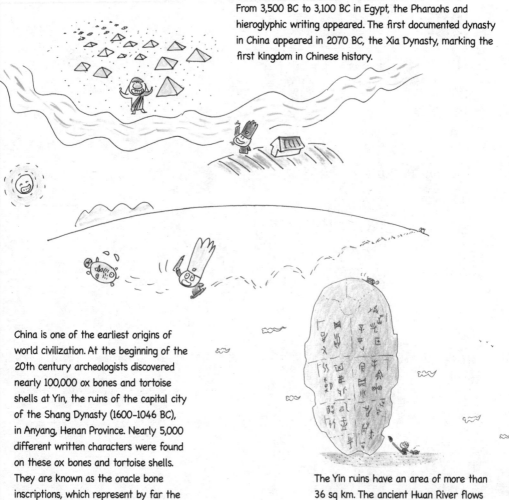

China is one of the earliest origins of world civilization. At the beginning of the 20th century archeologists discovered nearly 100,000 ox bones and tortoise shells at Yin, the ruins of the capital city of the Shang Dynasty (1600-1046 BC), in Anyang, Henan Province. Nearly 5,000 different written characters were found on these ox bones and tortoise shells. They are known as the oracle bone inscriptions, which represent by far the earliest understandable Chinese written characters.

The Yin ruins have an area of more than 36 sq km. The ancient Huan River flows through the city. The various buildings are rationally distributed. The city contains a palace area, an area of mausoleums for kings, a common cemetery, handicraft workshops, residential areas for common people and residential areas for slaves. Besides inscriptions on ox bones and tortoise shells, also excavated were large quantities of bronzeware, jade artifacts and pottery, as well as sacrificial pits where slaves were ceremonially sacrificed. The Yin ruins are on the UNESCO's World Heritage List.

Yin

Unified Country with Different Peoples Formed

The first emperor in Chinese history was the king of Qin named Ying Zheng. In 221 BC, Ying Zheng established the first unified, centralized multi-ethnic feudal country in Chinese history, the Qin Dynasty (221-206 BC), and called himself "the First Emperor."

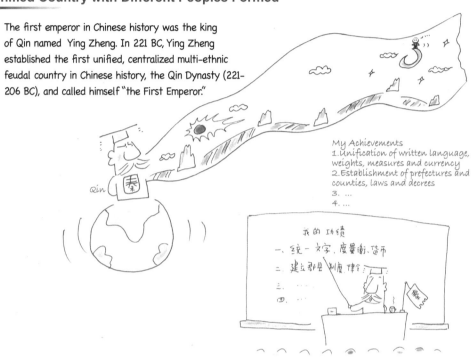

My Achievements
1. Unification of written language, weights, measures and currency
2. Establishment of prefectures and counties, laws and decrees
3. ...
4. ...

Qi   Chu   Yan   Zhao   Wei   Han

Qin

Horse (马)

Peace (安)

The First Emperor of Qin unified the written language, weights, measures, and currency. The system of prefectures and counties, laws and decrees were established, while direct roads were built between different places. The feudalist state structure established by the Qin emperor continued to be followed for more than 2,000 years after the establishment of the Qin Dynasty.

Your Majesty, now this is even more convenient.

19

Ancient Chinese people believed in the soul, that humans after death would live in another world. Therefore, the First Emperor of Qin ordered large numbers of people to build a mausoleum for him. In 210 BC, the First Emperor of Qin died and he was buried at the center of the mausoleum. There are many pits in the mausoleum, one of them filled with the now-famous terracotta warriors and horses.

Almost at the same time as the mausoleum construction, the First Emperor of Qin had the Great Wall built in the hilly terrains of northern China. The Great Wall is a comprehensive defense system of different defensive structures, including walls, passes, watchtowers, castles and fortresses.

Dialogue between the East and the West

After the short-lived Qin Dynasty, the Han Dynasty (206 BC-220 AD) was established in China. The Han period is regarded as a prosperous and tolerant historical time. Its agricultural technology and tools led the world at that time. The silk produced then was exquisite. Papermaking technology and the compass were invented during the Han Dynasty.

Western Regions

西域 Go!

Wait!

At that time, there were 36 kingdoms distributed in valleys and oases to the northwest of the Han, in an area collectively known as the "Western Regions." Han Emperor Wu (156-87 BC) appointed Zhang Qian as an envoy from Chang'an to visit the Western Regions. The diplomatic gates were thus opened, connecting the "Silk Road" across Europe and Asia.

22

迎外商来华

观光通商玩乐...

Chang'an

Foreign merchants are welcome in China! Please feel free to travel around and do trade!

After Zhang Qian, camel caravans of different countries carried Chinese silk to as far as the Mediterranean, where it was eagerly welcomed. Treasures of the West were also brought to China. Thus the Han Dynasty in the east and Romans in the west, as two of the strongest empires in the world, were connected.

The collapse of the Han Dynasty was followed by about 400 years of turmoil. Then, again China became a unified great empire. At first the Sui Dynasty (581–618) was established, followed by the Tang Dynasty (618–907). The Tang became a major empire in the world, with its famed prosperity, long history and vibrant international exchanges.

400 years of war and chaos

Han Dynasty

Sui Dynasty

Tang Dynasty

The silk products of the Tang Dynasty represented the highest level of textile production in the world. The ceramics industry also quickly developed. The Tang exported silks and ceramics, trading with other countries of advanced technology and culture.

The giant panda, considered a national treasure in China, is loved by many for its air of charming naivety. Giant pandas are given to other countries as special gifts from the Chinese, becoming special envoys in the exchanges between east and west.

city

Gradual Transformation of Agricultural Society

Ancient Chinese civilization was an agricultural
civilization characterized by clan networks. Men farmed
while women weaved in each family, which was a self-
sufficient unit. It was the ideal situation for rural
families. Men could gain official positions and respect
through learning and passing imperial civil examinations.

The Song Dynasty (960-1279) was an important historical period for social, economic and cultural development in China. Rapid urban development and a prosperous commodity economy raised the status of newly emerging urban residents. The traditional agricultural society was gradually transformed.

看 中國

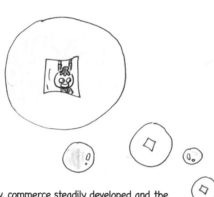

During the Song Dynasty, commerce steadily developed and the capital city Kaifeng became a prosperous commercial city. The status of merchants was elevated. This trend was more obvious in the Ming and Qing dynasties. Handicraft industries from the Song to Qing dynasties prospered, leading to China's prolonged favorable balance of foreign trade. The silk products varied in types, and porcelain became favored products in the West. The sea trade route from the Song Dynasty became known as the "Porcelain Road."

In ancient times, cities had strong political and military functions. But during the Song Dynasty, because of the development of the commodity economy, the city's status as a regional economic center was greatly strengthened. Furthermore, cities characterized by handicrafts (such as Jingdezhen) or trade (such as Quanzhou) flourished, making the city's role in economy more and more important.

The Forbidden City

The Palace Museum, also known as the "Forbidden City," was the imperial palace of the Ming and Qing dynasties, and is the largest surviving palace complex in the world. It was built from 1406 to 1420 under the rule of Ming Emperor Zhu Di.

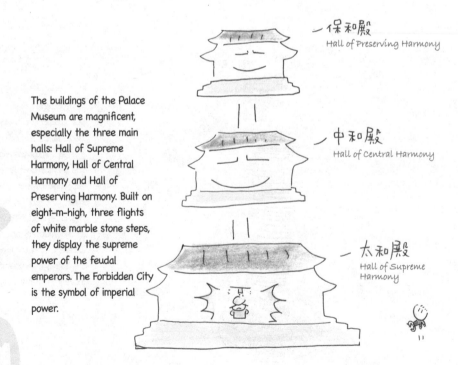

保和殿
Hall of Preserving Harmony

中和殿
Hall of Central Harmony

太和殿
Hall of Supreme Harmony

The buildings of the Palace Museum are magnificent, especially the three main halls: Hall of Supreme Harmony, Hall of Central Harmony and Hall of Preserving Harmony. Built on eight-m-high, three flights of white marble stone steps, they display the supreme power of the feudal emperors. The Forbidden City is the symbol of imperial power.

角楼 Watchtower

Gate of Divine Prowess 神武门

Watchtower 角楼

御花园
Imperial Gardens

乾清宫
Palace of Heavenly Purity

乾清门（皇上宿舍）
Gate of Heavenly Purity (Imperial Residence)

九龙壁
Nine Dragon Screen

保和殿（餐厅兼考场）
Hall of Preserving Harmony (Dining Room and Examination Hall)

中和殿（休息厅）
Hall of Central Harmony (Rest lounge)

太和殿（皇上办公室）
Hall of Supreme Harmony (Emperor's office)

Welcome!!
Hello!!

太和门
Gate of Supreme Harmony

角楼 Watchtower

角楼 Watchtower

午门 Meridian Gate

筒子河
筒子河
Palace Moat
Palace Moat

五色土社稷坛
Altar of Earth and Grain

端门
Upright Gate

太庙 Temple of the Imperial Ancestors

天安门
Gate of Heavenly Peace (Tiananmen)

This is all mine!
都是我的……

風上,太♯了你!!

All Hail Your Majesty!

From the 17th to 18th centuries, the famous Emperor Kangxi (1654-1722) of the Qing Dynasty (1616-1911) unified China with Taiwan, checked the expansion of tsarist Russia, and formulated a complete set of laws and regulations in which the central government authorized the leaders of Tibet. Under Emperor Kangxi's reign, the land area of China totaled more than 11 million sq km.

But the Qing Dynasty began to decline at the beginning of the 19th century. In 1840, because of China's refusal to the opium trade, the First Opium War broke out between China and Britain. China was defeated in this war between the ancient agricultural empire in the East and the newly emerging industrial empire in the West, and was forced to cede territory and pay reparations. The year 1842 became a turning point in Chinese history, when China became a semi-colonial society.

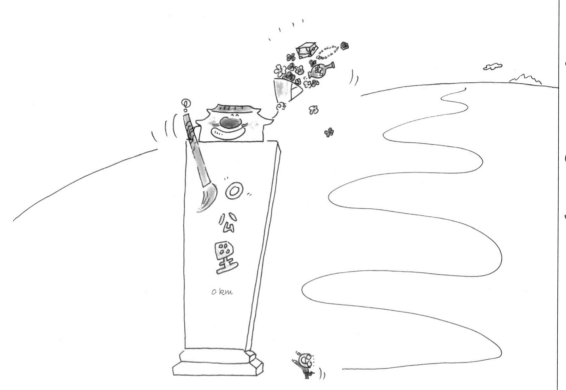

The Palace Museum was an imperial palace,
and is now a museum. The Palace Museum
is a cultural, artistic, social and historic
landmark of the Chinese people.

Beijing, a Modern International Metropolis

In 1949, the People's Republic of China (PRC) was established. In 60 years, great changes have taken place in this country. At present, the PRC has entered a stage of stable development, following impressive achievements in all fields. There have been notable changes in people's styles of living. Residents in Beijing and Shanghai live a life not very different from those living in London or New York. But in more remote villages, many traditional ways of life are still kept.

Beijing, the capital, is China's political, economic and cultural center. Combining ancient culture with modern civilization, Beijing, a city with more than 3,000 years of history and over 850 years as the capital, is a famous historical and cultural center in the world and one of the four ancient capitals in China.

History has granted Beijing a precious cultural heritage including: the Great Wall, the Summer Palace, the Palace Museum and the Temple of Heaven ...

Today's Beijing has become a modern international metropolis. Beijing's Capital International Airport, the National Stadium (aka the Bird's Nest), the Water Cube, the National Center for the Performing Arts, CCTV Tower and high-rises along Chang'an Boulevard all brim with metropolitan modernity. Financial Street has already become the financial management center of China. The Central Business District (CBD) is the symbol of Beijing's opening-up and economic strength.

看

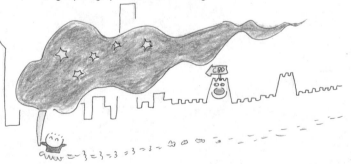

中國

The traditional *hutong* (alleys) and *siheyuan* (quadrangle) courtyard residences in the capital are historic symbols of Beijing life. *Hutong* are unique ancient city alleys in Beijing, where *siheyuan* are situated along the *hutong*. Quadrangles are traditional residential compounds with houses around a courtyard.

Beijing is also the city where avant-garde and contemporary artists live. In Beijing's northeast in a deserted factory complex, since 2002 many artists and cultural agencies have rented the buildings, turning them into art galleries, art centers, art studios, design companies, restaurants and bars. This district, now called Beijing's 798 Art Zone, has become an exhibition center for China's culture and arts, especially avant-garde arts.

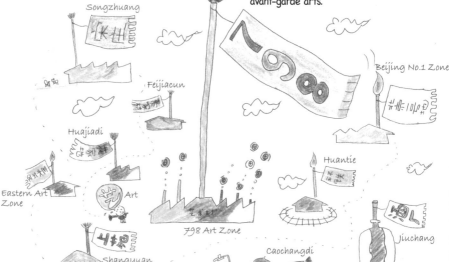

Songzhuang

Feijiacun

Beijing No.1 Zone

Huajiadi

Huantie

Eastern Art Zone

Art

798 Art Zone

Jiuchang

Shangyuan

Caochangdi

The BIG Book of CHINA

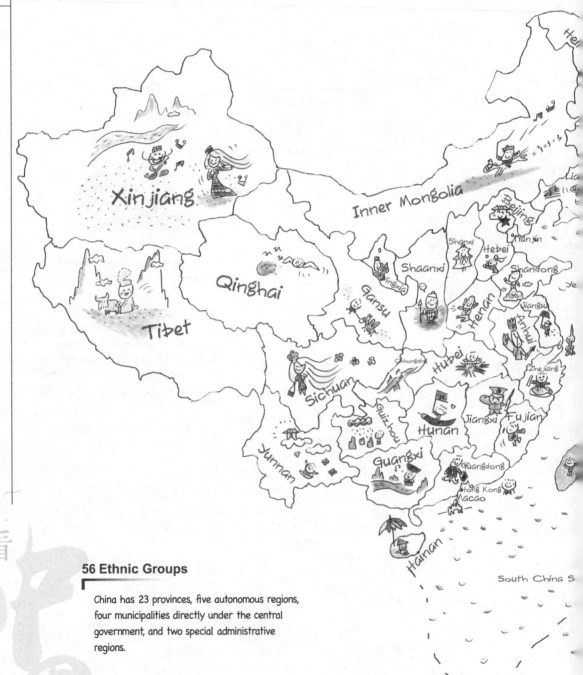

56 Ethnic Groups

China has 23 provinces, five autonomous regions,
four municipalities directly under the central
government, and two special administrative
regions.

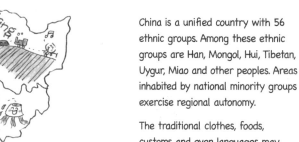

China is a unified country with 56 ethnic groups. Among these ethnic groups are Han, Mongol, Hui, Tibetan, Uygur, Miao and other peoples. Areas inhabited by national minority groups exercise regional autonomy.

The traditional clothes, foods, customs and even languages may differ greatly, but altogether the 56 ethnic groups form a colorful large family. More than 90% of the Chinese population is Han. Of the other 55 minorities, the Zhuang has the largest population, of 16 million, while the Lhoba ethnic group has the smallest population, of about 3,000.

The population of China is over 1.3 billion. The country has adopted family planning and population growth control policies. This is not only necessary for China, but also makes a major contribution toward global stability and development.

NO. 1

Records for China

Like other countries, China holds many world records.

Tiananmen Square is the world's largest square. Located in central Beijing, Tiananmen Square covers an area of 440,000 sq m, big enough for a gathering of one million people.

The Great Wall is the world's longest wall. The Great Wall was built in the Qin Dynasty over 2,000 years ago. Now the Great Wall has a length of about 6,700 km.

Forbidden City is the world's largest imperial palace. Also known as the Palace Museum, it covers an area of 725,000 sq m, with total building area of 155,000 sq m. The Forbidden City is surrounded by 10m-high walls and a 52m-wide moat.

The Potala Palace is the world's highest palace. The Potala Palace is located in Lhasa, capital city of the Tibet Autonomous Region. Covering an area of 100,000 sq m, the Potala Palace is acclaimed as one of the top 10 earthen buildings in the world.

Loess Plateau is the world's largest loess topography. The Loess Plateau covers an area of about 300,000 sq km. The main part of the Plateau is covered by loess or yellow earth. Eroded by water over a long time, unique natural scenery is formed characterized by crisscrossing gullies.

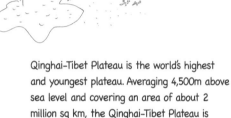

Yarlung Zangbo River is the world's highest river. The Yarlung Zangbo River originates from the snow on the northern slopes of the middle section of Mt. Himalayas. The part of the river that flows inside Chinese territory is 2,057 km long, with a drainage area of 240,480 sq km.

Qinghai-Tibet Plateau is the world's highest and youngest plateau. Averaging 4,500m above sea level and covering an area of about 2 million sq km, the Qinghai-Tibet Plateau is considered the "roof of the world."

Mount Himalayas is the highest mountain range in the world. The highest peak of this mountain range, Mount Qomolangma, aka Mount Everest, standing at 8844.43 m, is the highest peak in the world.

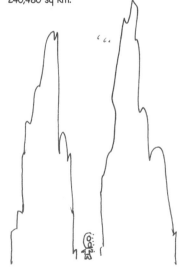

The 504.6 km-long Yarlung Zangbo Canyon is the world's deepest and longest canyon. The most precipitous core part of the canyon is 240 km long, with an average depth over 5,000 m. Its deepest spot is near Namjagbarwa Peak, going down 5,382 m.

Turpan Basin in Xinjiang is the world's lowest basin. It is 154 m below sea level.

Beijing-Hangzhou Grand Canal is the world's longest manmade waterway. It is 1,794 km long, running from Beijing in the north to Hangzhou in southeast China.

Qinghai-Tibet Railway is the world's longest plateau railway. The Qinghai-Tibet Railway consists of the section from Xining in Qinghai Province to Golmud and the section from Golmud to Lhasa, with a total length of 1,956 km.

The Silk Road is the oldest trade route between the East and the West. The Silk Road originated before 100 BC.

Giant Stone Buddha in Leshan County is the world's largest stone statue of Buddha. The Stone Buddha is 71 m high, with the head alone being 14.7 m high.

Ginkgo is one of the oldest tree species in the world. Ginkgo was one of the vigorous tree species from as early as 250 million years ago when dinosaurs roamed the earth.

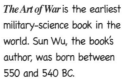

The Art of War is the earliest military-science book in the world. Sun Wu, the book's author, was born between 550 and 540 BC.

Records of the Historian is the earliest biographical literature in the world. *Records of the Historian* is a spectacular history book, as well as a famous biographical book. The book comprehensively records 3,000 years of China's political, economic and cultural conditions from ancient times to the early Han Dynasty.

41

The most neighboring countries,
the most friends

邻国最多… 朋友最多

China possesses the largest number of neighboring
countries in the world. The land border of China
totals 2,280,000 km. China is bordered by 14
countries on land, and has eight neighboring
countries by sea.

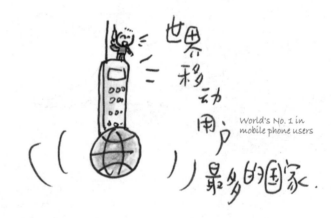

世界移动用户

World's No. 1 in
mobile phone users

最多的国家.

China has the largest number of mobile phone
users in the world. There are 640 million mobile
phone users in China. China also has the largest
GSM and CDMA network capacity in the world.

看

02

Eastern Wisdom

Chinese culture is characterized by its richness and tolerance. With a focus on handling problems in daily life, Confucian philosophy has won the respect of Chinese people; and with its pursuit of a freer life, the philosophy of Laozi and Zhuangzi has served as a balm for people's souls. A panoramic culture has originated from this historical environment of dynamic thinking.

Confucius' Active Pursuit of Life

Confucius (or Kongzi, 551–479 BC) was
an educator, thinker and the founder
of Confucianism in the late Spring and
Autumn Period. Legend has it that he
had 3,000 disciples, 72 of whom were
distinguished scholars. His teachings were
compiled by his disciples into a collection
titled *Analects of Confucius*, known as the
classic of Confucianism.

The core of Confucius theory is *ren* (benevolence) and *li* (rites), signifying that people should live in peace and harmony with each other and treat each other with due respect. Today, his thoughts still have a great impact on the character and conduct of Chinese people.

Benevolence

Benevolent government

Confucius was concerned about people's livelihood and advocated benevolent government. At the age of 63, Confucius had just spent nine years taking his students to tour many kingdoms in an attempt to sell his political ideas to the rulers. Experiencing all sorts of hardships, however, he received no appointment from those dukes or princes and even nearly lost his life. But Confucius was still optimistic and upheld his dreams. Sometimes he even attempted the impossible.

Confucius stressed *zhong* (loyalty) and *shu* (forbearance) in human relations. *Zhong* represents that one should treat others with loyalty and honesty, and be wholeheartedly devoted to one's duty; while *shu* implies that one should put oneself in the place of another, and "do not do to others what you do not want done to yourself." Showing a prudent attitude to the Mandate of Heaven, he attached more importance to human power.

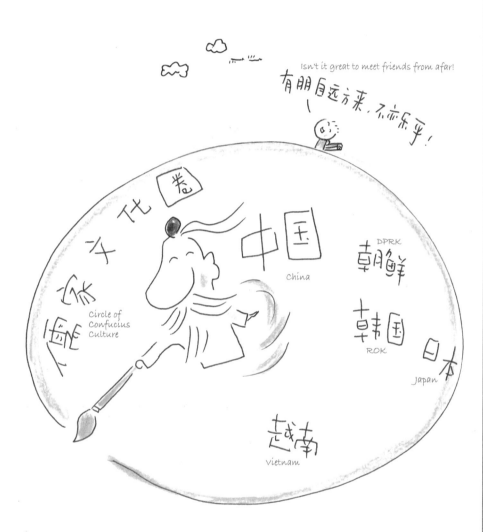

Isn't it great to meet friends from afar!

有朋自远方来, 不亦乐乎!

儒家文化圈
Circle of Confucius Culture

中国
China

朝鲜
DPRK

韩国
ROK

日本
Japan

越南
Vietnam

Confucius and Confucianism have had far-reaching impact over many Asian countries, including China, Korea, Japan and Vietnam, which constitute the "circle of Confucian culture."

Concept of *Wuwei* (effortless action) in Laozi and Zhuangzi's Philosophy

It is generally believed that *Dao De Jing* (*Tao Te Ching, Book of the Way and Virtue*) was written by the philosopher Laozi (born around 600 BC) in the Spring and Autumn Period. Though the text consists of only around 5,000 Chinese characters, it is an important source for China's indigenous religion of Daoism, exerting a significant influence on ancient Chinese philosophy, science, politics and religion.

看中國

The core of Laozi's philosophy is *wuwei* (effortless action). In his view, everything has its own pattern of movement, i.e., the *dao* (way). People should look for and follow the *dao*, instead of violating it.

Zhuangzi's outlook on life is reflected in his dialogue with Huizi while strolling along the dam of the Hao Waterfall. Zhuangzi said, "See how the minnows come out and dart around where they please! That's what fish really enjoy!" In Zhuangzi's eyes, "the Happiness of Fish" contains inherent reason. He looked at the fish as one who attains enlightenment, and water as the *dao* (way). Without covetous desire or dispute, the carefree fish represents Zhuangzi's attitude toward life.

The Inconstant Zhouyi

Zhouyi (*Book of Changes*), also known as the *I Ching*, took initial shape more than 3,000 years ago, and had far-reaching repercussions all over China. Confucius read the *Book of Changes* so many times that the ropes linking the bamboo slips on which it was written snapped from overuse. However, no one since the Qin and Han dynasties has a complete comprehension of the text.

According to the book, everything in the universe is continually changing. "Yi" means "to change," while yin and yang are the two opposing factors of change.

The book attaches equal importance to an enterprising spirit and magnanimous tolerance. Its text reads: "As heaven maintains vigor through movement, a virtuous person should constantly strive for self-perfection. As the earth's condition is receptive devotion, a virtuous person should hold the outer world with a broad mind."

Book of Changes

After experiencing several thousand years of ups and downs, the *Book of Changes* has become a source of Chinese civilization.

The Art of War and Military Wisdom

The Art of War is the most famed Chinese military treatise. The core idea of the book is that one side achieves victory by making surprise moves, creating favorable conditions while strictly keeping secret actual deployments, thus gaining the initiative in war.

The Art of War

Aiya (Oh no)!

Know yourself and the enemy ...

According to the book's author Sunzi, war is of vital importance to the state, as a matter of its survival or destruction. Hence, it is imperative that it be studied thoroughly. The book reveals the laws of war, i.e., by knowing both yourself and the enemy, you can win 100 battles without a single loss. Sunzi advocated collecting military information on the enemy by various means, to gain the initiative in war.

In a strict sense, Sunzi was against war. According to him, war causes a drain on resources; hence, victory without fighting is best. To seize the enemy without fighting would be a complete triumph. Hence, he advocated gaining victory through strategy. Seizing the enemy without fighting represents advanced humanitarian thinking in the ancient history of war.

The Art of War

Sunzi's military ideas produced a great impact on Chinese militarists, politicians and thinkers. Praised as the most successful book on military strategy, *The Art of War* has been translated into dozens of languages and spread all over the world.

Vibrant Chinese Characters

Chinese is the common language used in China, and Chinese characters (*hanzi*) are the ideograms used in writing Chinese. Invented by Chinese people, Chinese characters represent the oldest ideographs in the world passed down to this day. The script's history can be traced back to over 4,000 years ago. There are innumerable Chinese characters, but only about 3,500 are in common use.

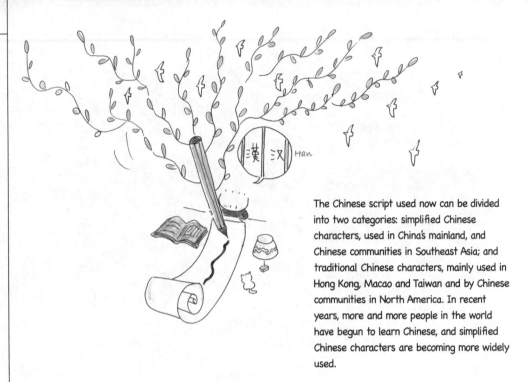

The Chinese script used now can be divided into two categories: simplified Chinese characters, used in China's mainland, and Chinese communities in Southeast Asia; and traditional Chinese characters, mainly used in Hong Kong, Macao and Taiwan and by Chinese communities in North America. In recent years, more and more people in the world have begun to learn Chinese, and simplified Chinese characters are becoming more widely used.

As the foundation of the Chinese script, pictographs make up a portion of Chinese characters, depicting objects' shapes and emphasizing their features, like 日 (*rì*) for "sun" and 月 (*yuè*) for "moon." For example, in 旦 (*dàn*) for "dawn," the upper part signifies the sun while the lower part represents the horizon. Together they create a picture of the sun rising slowly from the horizon, thus indicating "daybreak" and "beginning."

永和九年歲在癸丑暮春之初

會于會稽山陰之蘭亭脩禊事

也群賢畢至少長咸集此地

有峻領茂林脩竹又有清流激

湍暎帶左右引以為流觴曲水

列坐其次雖無絲竹管弦之盛

一觴一詠亦足以暢敘幽情是

日也天朗氣清惠風和暢仰

觀宇宙之大俯察品類之盛

所以遊目騁懷足以極視聽之

娛信可樂也夫人之相與俯仰

好字！
Great strokes!

The unique art of calligraphy took shape as Chinese characters were being written out. This is usually done with an ink brush, made of goat or weasel hair. The soft tip dipped in ink can create all sorts of surprises. There are many eminent calligraphers throughout Chinese history.

The evolution of Chinese characters is interesting.

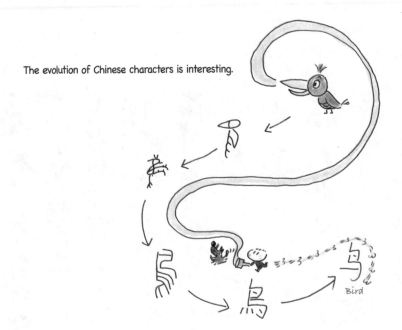

Bird

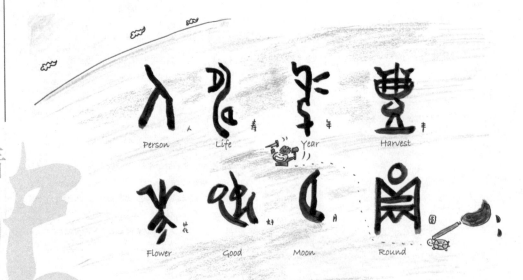

Person

Life

Year

Harvest

Flower

Good

Moon

Round

看

Gorgeous Bronzes

China's Bronze Age began about 4,000 years ago, spanning over 1,500 years from the Xia, Shang and Zhou dynasties to the Spring and Autumn Period. Numerous excavated bronze artifacts bear political, religious and cultural connotations, and possess remarkable artistic value.

Harvest

The Simuwu *ding*, a sacrificial vessel for the royal family, represents the highest achievement in bronzeware casting of the Shang Dynasty (c. 1600–c. 1100 BC). The whole *ding* measures 133 cm in height and 875 kg in weight, and its opening is 110 cm long and 78 cm wide. It has a rectangular belly, with two straight ears above and four feet below. The heavy *ding*, decorated with beautiful patterns, is the world's largest bronze artifact ever excavated.

Ruins of the ancient Kingdom of Shu during the Shang Dynasty were discovered Near Sanxingdui Village in Guanghan, Sichuan Province. A 163.5cm-high bronze figure was excavated in a pit of sacrificial offerings. Standing on a platform, the dignified figure likely depicts a king of the ancient Kingdom of Shu. Another striking find was a large bronze mask used for sacrificial purposes, possessing the mysterious power of religion.

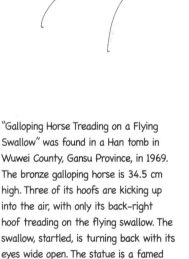

你到底在想什么？

What are you thinking about?

你怎么不告诉我

Why won't you tell me?

"Galloping Horse Treading on a Flying Swallow" was found in a Han tomb in Wuwei County, Gansu Province, in 1969. The bronze galloping horse is 34.5 cm high. Three of its hoofs are kicking up into the air, with only its back-right hoof treading on the flying swallow. The swallow, startled, is turning back with its eyes wide open. The statue is a famed masterpiece displaying a rare swiftness.

漢

Han

The Smiling Buddha

Buddhism was introduced into China in the 1st century AD. It has produced a great impact on Chinese culture, inspiring large numbers of Buddhist artworks. Most giant sculptures in China are Buddhist statues. These mainly include statues in Datong's Yungang Grottoes, Luoyang's Longmen Grottoes, Dunhuang's Mogao Caves, Leshan's giant Buddha and Chongqing's Dazu Rock Carvings. The four most famous rock caves with fantastic works of sculpture in China are the Mogao, Yungang, Longmen and Maijishan grottoes.

Mogao Grottoes, also known as Caves of the Thousand Buddhas, are located 25 km southeast of Dunhuang, in Gansu Province, on the eastern slope of Mount Mingsha (Echoing Sands), with five stories stretching about 1,600 m from south to north. Construction of the Buddhist cave shrines began in 366 AD. Created through generations of efforts, the grand Mogao Grottoes feature distinctive architecture, painted sculptures and murals, as the largest treasure-house of best-preserved Buddhist art.

Beautiful flying Apsaras dancing in the air are often seen in the murals of the Mogao Caves. The statue for the city of Dunhuang is also an Apsara playing a stringed pipa instrument behind its back. With graceful lines and unfolded posture, the statue presents an indescribably free world.

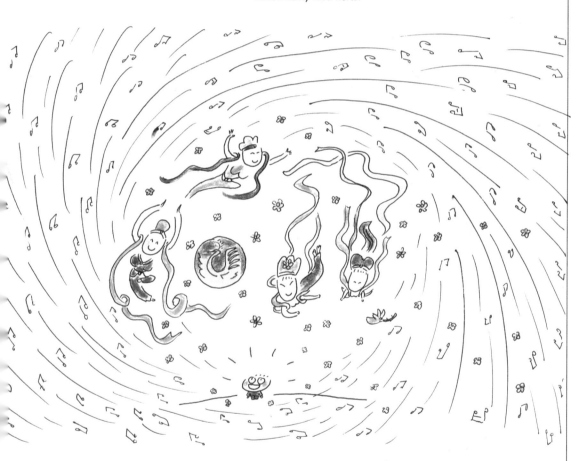

16 m

10 cm

The Maijishan Grottoes' construction began in 384 AD. Maijishan is known for the elegant clay sculptures. With the largest sculpture 16 m high and the smallest only over 10 cm, the Maijishan Grottoes feature sculptures of different periods.

Sculptures in the Maijishan Grottoes reveal remarkable secular trends. Except for the earliest ones, most of the Buddha sculptures are looking down with gentle and affable faces at all living beings. They are more like common people rather than gods in the heavens.

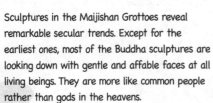

The Longmen Grottoes are located in the southern outskirts of Luoyang, Henan Province. Two mountains stand facing each other, with the Yi River flowing between them. On the mountain cliffs were carved more than 110,000 statues, depicting Buddhist sculptural arts from the late Northern Wei to Tang dynasties (493 to 907).

Fengxian Temple is the largest grotto in the Longmen Grottoes. In the center of the temple is the statue of Vairochana Buddha. This giant Buddha statue is 17.14 m high and magnificent in appearance. Slightly bowing his head, the smiling Buddha wears a serene expression.

The Dazu Rock Carvings are located in southwestern China's Chongqing Municipality, found within the steep hillsides throughout Dazu County. Carvings here, completed from the 9th to 13th centuries, represent the height of China's later grottoes.

The statue of "Sakyamuni Entering Nirvana," also called the Sleeping Buddha, is the largest of the Dazu rock carvings. With a total length of 31 m, the sleeping Buddha is lying on his right side, with feet facing south. With an unruffled expression, the Buddha looks as if asleep.

Eastern Attire

Traditional Chinese dress is characterized by four elements: first, jacket with front buttons, and most female garments having the buttons diagonally on the right or left, showing a graceful charm; second, straight (mandarin) collar, i.e., erect collar open at the center front; third, raglan sleeves, i.e., sleeves extending in one piece with the garment; and fourth, butterfly buttons, composed of knots and button loops. In addition, brocade satin is commonly used to make traditional Chinese clothing.

At the APEC meeting held in 2001, all leaders present wore Chinese attire, drawing worldwide attention.

The modern *qipao* (or cheongsam) began developing in the 1920s, and flourished in Shanghai in the 1930s. Its style has changed with the times, including the size of the collar, length of sleeves and openings, all revealing the graceful female figure. Since the 1930s, the *qipao* has become the standard dress for Chinese women, serving as formal attire for social occasions and diplomatic activities.

Ink-wash Painting Expressing the Heart

Ink-wash painting plays a representative role in
Chinese fine arts, similar to oil painting in Western
art. It is a unique form of painting: the artist paints
on soft xuan paper or silk using a brush dipped in
ink and pigment; and with no emphasis on color, it is
usually a "world of black and white" on white paper
or silk, filled with rich connotations.

Western oil paintings are very different from ink-wash paintings in China.

Chinese ink-and-wash paintings create graceful artistic concepts in simple black and white ...

看

Color was frequently used in early Chinese paintings, but ink-wash painting became dominant after famed Tang poet Wang Wei. The techniques of ink-wash painting grew most rapidly from the 10th to 14th centuries, when a large number of masters emerged.

Ink-wash paintings usually overstep formal resemblance, going against the perspective principle, thus totally different from Western painting. Chinese ink-wash painting takes artistic conception as the soul.

Ancient Chinese painters liked drawing Chinese plum blossoms, orchids, bamboo and chrysanthemum, esteemed as symbols of noble and pure character. Zheng Banqiao, a mid-Qing-dynasty painter, excelled at drawing bamboo. His masterpiece *Ink Bamboo* reveals the painter's inner world of pride and aloofness.

Besides the picture, (name) seals and poems are commonly seen as part of ink-wash paintings. Hence, ink-wash painting is a genre of unified art of picture, poetry, calligraphy and seal.

Guqin and *Kunqu*

A large horizontal plucked instrument, the *guqin* has the longest history among all Chinese musical instruments. With a range of over 100 harmonics, which is probably the highest among all musical instruments in the world, the *guqin* is capable of expressing artistic creativity, from simple yet profound to powerful and elementary.

Guqin has been especially favored by scholars. Rather like wearing jade, which can not be dispensed with even for a moment, the playing of *guqin* is closely related to the cultivation of one's character. The *guqin* is the embodiment of noble refinement. Playing the *guqin* is considered an important way to refine a person's sentiments and purify the mind.

Kunqu Opera originated from Kunshan, in Jiangsu Province. It is so gentle, exquisite, sentimental and melodious, that it is commonly called *shuimoqiang* (millstone music). The performance is accompanied by stringed instruments, vertical bamboo flute and wood clappers.

The Peony Pavilion written by Tang Xianzu (1550–1616) is a classic *Kunqu* opera and has brought perpetual fame to the opera. It is a love story between Du Liniang, daughter of a senior official and the scholar Liu Mengmei. With refined and subtle lyrics, *The Peony Pavilion* creates a scene as beautiful as the poetry of Tang and Song dynasties and Yuan operas.

Kunqu is known as the "mother" of 100 operas, because of its far-reaching influence on Peking Opera and other local operas.

73

看
中
國

74

Brilliant Peking Opera

As China's national opera, Peking Opera is a harmonious combination of "*chang*" (singing), "*nian*" (dialogue), "*zuo*" (acting) and "*da*" (martial arts). It is the most popular and influential opera style in China. Peking Opera was named for its origins in Peking (now called Beijing).

The performance of Peking Opera features virtuality. For instance, the performer holds and wields a horsewhip, while turning round pretending to ride a horse. This virtuality gives the performer a wide world to play in, and offering much to fascinate the audience's imagination.

Song: "singing drama" refers to performing the songs of an opera

"唱戏"就是指戏是唱来的

Movement: "acting" features the body movements, poses and facial expressions

"做"指的是舞蹈性很强的表演动作身段、姿势及面部表情.

京剧中的"念"是指带有音乐性的说话,也叫"道白"。具有节奏感和韵律感,美妙悦耳.

Speech: "reciting" the melodic and rhythmic stage dialogues

"打"是舞蹈性很强的表演形式。一类是徒手格斗。一类是使用兵器格斗.

Combat: "fighting" through dance-like martial arts either barehanded or with weapons

好戏开场

The show's on!

Sheng (male)
生（男人）

旦（女人）
Dan (female)

净
（威猛的男人
别称"大花脸"）
Jing (powerful painted-face male)

丑
（丑角
别称"小花脸"）
Chou (clown)

The show's over ...
曲终人散....

Roles mainly fall into four categories in Peking Opera: *Sheng* (male), *Dan* (female), *Jing* (powerful painted-face male) and *Chou* (clown). The "Four Famous *Dan* Performers" are Mei Lanfang, Cheng Yanqiu, Shang Xiaoyun and Xun Huisheng. Mei Lanfang is the most representative Peking Opera performer.

看

On the Peking Opera stage, besides magnificent costumes, the dazzling facial makeup is also striking. The painted face is a special feature of Peking Opera, usually on roles for *Jing* and *Chou*, and the most often used colors are red, yellow and black.

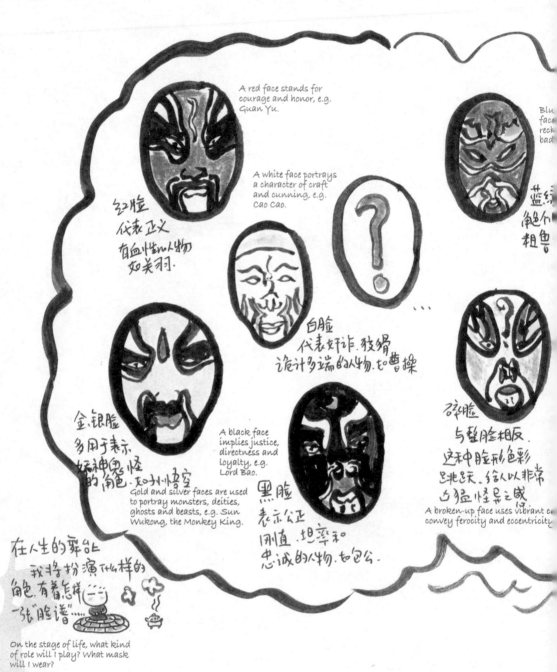

A red face stands for courage and honor, e.g. Guan Yu.

红脸
代表正义
有血性的人物
如关羽.

A white face portrays a character of craft and cunning, e.g. Cao Cao.

Blu
face
reck
bad

蓝绿
脸
鲁莽
粗鲁

白脸
代表奸诈.狡猾
诡计多端的人物.如曹操

金,银脸
多用于表示
妖神鬼怪
的角色.如孙悟空
Gold and silver faces are used to portray monsters, deities, ghosts and beasts, e.g. Sun Wukong, the Monkey King.

A black face implies justice, directness and loyalty, e.g. Lord Bao.

碎脸
与整脸相反
这种脸形色彩
显跳跃.给人以非常
凶猛怪异之感
A broken-up face uses vibrant c convey ferocity and eccentricity

黑脸
表示公正
刚直.坦率和
忠诚的人物.如包公.

在人生的舞台上
我将扮演怎样的
角色.有着怎样
一张"脸谱"...

On the stage of life, what kind of role will I play? What mask will I wear?

看

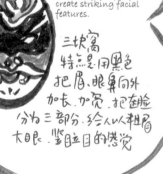

reen
ate
ss and

Cross-faces are usually military officials.

十字脸
此脸角色多为
武将.

A three-part face features three different color patches at the eyebrows, eyes and nose, stretching out from these points to create striking facial features.

三块窝
特点是用黑色
把眉、眼鼻向外
加长. 加宽. 把在脸
分为三部分. 给人以粗眉
大眼. 坚脸目的感觉

Facial makeup is important in portraying characters in Peking Opera. For example, red face stands for loyalty and bravery, while black implies rough boldness, and white, craftiness. A face with a patch of chalk on and around the nose implies an unimportant person, while unsymmetrical lines symbolize a deceitful man.

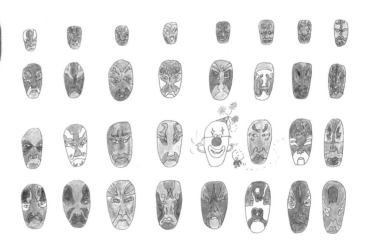

Chang'an Grand Theater

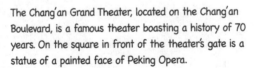

The Chang'an Grand Theater, located on the Chang'an
Boulevard, is a famous theater boasting a history of 70
years. On the square in front of the theater's gate is a
statue of a painted face of Peking Opera.

看

中

國

Kingdom of Poetry

The Tang Dynasty (618–907) is commonly recognized as the golden age of poetry. This was a period of power and prosperity. Culture became more open and tolerant during the Tang, stimulating the development of poetry. Out of this period emerged Li Bai, the great poet of the romantic school, and Du Fu who emphasized realism.

Du Fu lived through troubled years of war and rebellion. Therefore, he showed special concern for the people's sufferings. In a disconsolate mood, his poetry focused on people's livelihood.

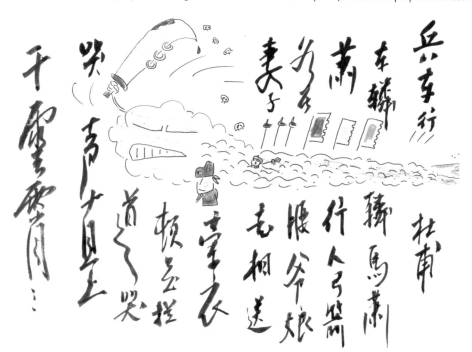

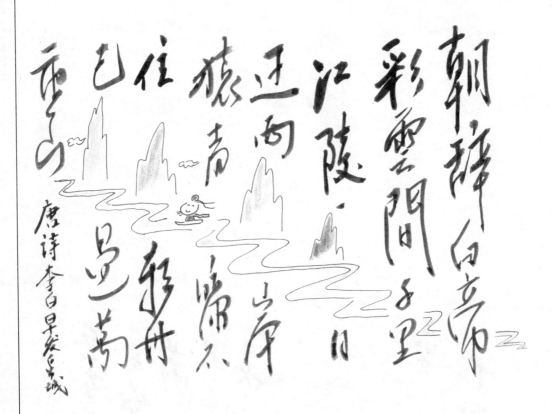

看中國

The style of Li Bai's poetry is totally different from that of Du Fu. Du Fu's poems give expression to Confucianist *ren* (benevolence), while Li Bai's poems pursuing freedom and detachment reflect the Daoist spiritual world.

安能摧眉
折腰事权贵
使我不得
开心颜

Ci poetry reached its peak in the Song Dynasty (960-1279). *Ci* goes by many names. Since it can be sung to music, it is called *ci* lyrics. As the lengths of lines differ, it is also known as "long-and-short-line verses." Outstanding *ci* composers of the Song Dynasty include Su Shi, Li Qingzhao and Xin Qiji.

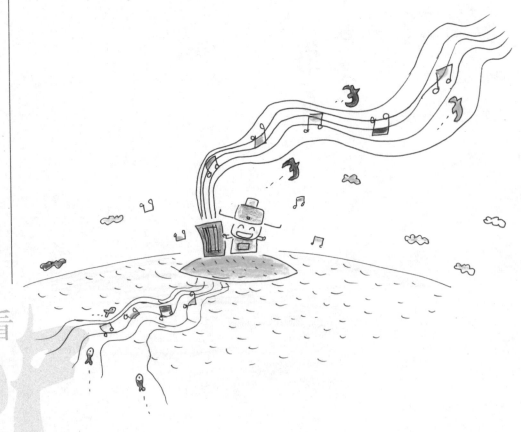

Four Classic Novels

The Tang and Song dynasties were known for their enduring poetry and *ci* (lyrics). The Ming and Qing dynasties saw the emergence of classical novels including historical romances, legends of heroes, stories of gods and demons, and fiction on manners and society. The representative works of these four types respectively are: *Three Kingdoms*, *Outlaws of the Marsh*, *Journey to the West* and *A Dream of Red Mansions*, generally referred to as China's "four classic novels."

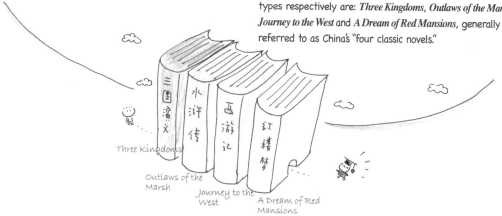

Three Kingdoms

Outlaws of the Marsh

Journey to the West

A Dream of Red Mansions

A Dream of Red Mansions is the greatest work of Chinese classical novels. It was written by Cao Xueqin (1724–1764) of the Qing Dynasty. The novel focuses on the tragic love story of Jia Baoyu, Lin Daiyu and Xue Baochai, and depicts the rise and fall of an aristocratic family in that era. It became a representative work of Chinese classical novels, and even led to the emergence of a distinct academic discipline — "Hongloumeng (Red) Studies."

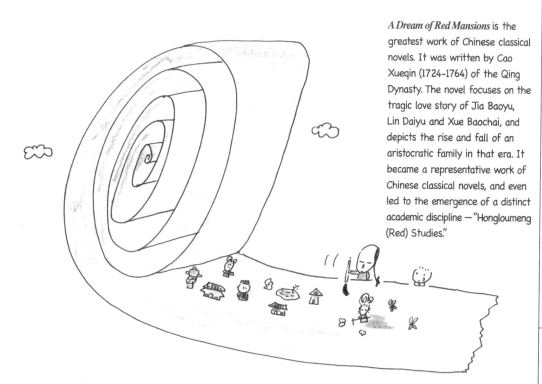

Wei

Shu

Wu

Let the games begin!

Three Kingdoms was a path-breaker for historical novels. By depicting political and military struggles during the Three Kingdoms Period (220–280), the book portrays some all-conquering heroes. The author of the novel is Luo Guanzhong (c.1330–1400).

Justice from Heaven

The author of *Outlaws of the Marsh* was Shi Nai'an (c.1296–1370). The book recounts the peasants' uprisings led by Song Jiang in the late Northern Song Dynasty (960–1127). At that time, driven to rebellion by tyrannical rulers, people had gathered at Mount Liangshan. The novel reproduces the entire process from the beginning to the failure of peasant uprisings against feudal society.

86

Journey to the West was written by Wu Cheng'en (1501–1582), a Ming Dynasty writer. It is the representative work of novels of gods and demons. The book tells the story of the journey westward by a Tang priest. Escorted by the Monkey King, they experience 81 disasters before finally reaching their destination and obtaining the sutras. The novel presents to readers a magnificent and colorful world of gods and demons.

The Monkey King
孙悟空

Xuanzang
唐僧

Pigsy
猪八戒

沙和尚
Sha Wujing

Cutting, bundling, plaiting, knitting, embroidery, carving, molding, painting

Folk Arts

China boasts a wide variety of arts and crafts which are renowned for their excellent workmanship. In terms of techniques, Chinese folk arts are categorized into: cutting, bundling, plaiting, knitting, embroidering, carving, molding, and painting. They all have strong local characteristics and diverse folk styles.

Chinese Knots. A typical Chinese knot is plaited using red and yellow silk thread. With graceful curves and elegant appeal, the auspicious or lucky ornaments passed on from generation to generation, for people's wishes and for prosperous life.

Papercuts. This ancient craft originates from the inspiration of daily life and physical labor. Common people use scissors to cut paper into various designs. Flowers, birds and fish and insects are familiar objects depicted in this art. Homophones and symbols are also used in auspicious designs, such as a boy sitting on a lotus (*lian*, sounds like Chinese for "successive," meaning one boy after another was born in the family), bat (*fu*, or "good fortune"), and roosters and goats (homophones for "*ji xiang*" meaning "good luck").

89

Peace and Prosperity   Years of Abundance

富貴吉祥   年年有餘

New Year Paintings. As a form of painting pasted up during the Spring Festival, (lunar) New Year Paintings have a history of several thousand years. The artisans first engrave the painting draft on a piece of wood-block, to which they then apply bright and joyful colors. Finally, they press sheets of colorful paper against the wood-block, creating a rubbing to complete the painting. Most of the designs are legendary figures, roly-poly children, or of social customs.

Kites. The kite was invented by the Chinese people over 2,000 years ago. Birds, insects or geometric patterns are subjects for kite designs. The materials used for making kites are mainly spun silk, paper, and bamboo strips. It is said that people first flew kites for good luck. When the kites reached so high as to touch the clouds, people would cut the string with knives, so the kites would disappear into the clouds. At this moment, people would shout, "bad luck is gone," repeatedly for good luck.

Jingtai cloisonné enamelware. Jingtai cloisonné enamel, reputed as a unique traditional handicraft of Beijing, gets its name from the fine blue-glaze variety produced during the Ming Dynasty's Jingtai reign (1450-1457). It uses red copper in various shapes as the base. The designs are inlaid with copper or gold filigree, and then filled with enamel. Production of this handicraft has to go through a process of firing, polishing and gilding.

91

Tang Tricolor-glazed Pottery. A type of glazed pottery with the dominant colors of yellow, white and green was very popular during the Tang Dynasty. It was later called Tang Tricolor-glazed Pottery, or *tangsancai*. It is famed for vibrant and true-to-life shapes, bright colors, and depictions of everyday life.

Suzhou embroidery. Suzhou embroidery is produced in south China's city of Suzhou. Since the Song Dynasty, the embroidery industry of Suzhou has been very prosperous. Various designs, such as mountains and rivers, pavilions, flowers and birds, and figures, can be reproduced in Suzhou embroidery. It also absorbs the strong points of the Western painting in creating contrast and three-dimensional effects. Suzhou embroidery possesses great artistic appeal.

Shadow play is an ancient form of storytelling and entertainment using opaque, often articulated figures in front of an illuminated backdrop to create the illusion of moving images.

Excuse me, how do I get to the "Bird's Nest"?

Paper heads attached to the bodies of shadow-puppet characters: identify these figures as male, female, clown or other roles.
Shadow play has been a popular art in Chinese folk culture for over 2,000 years. It integrates traditional elements of opera, music, literature, carving and painting.

In temple fairs — the Chinese version of carnival—dragon dance, lion dance, stilt walking, etc dazzled the audience.

好
Bravo!

好!!
Great show!

Delicious Foods

Chinese people like to use chopsticks when eating meals. Chopsticks are usually made of a pair of thin wooden sticks, and are very convenient and useful. China covers a vast territory, hence a wide variety of Chinese foods with different yet wonderful flavors. For instance, Huaiyang cuisine is light and pleasing to the eye, whereas Sichuan cuisine is known for its appetizing, spicy and strong flavors.

Sometimes, a cooking process can resemble an acrobatics performance. Cooks making Shanxi cut (or sliced) noodles possess special skills. The cook stands a meter away from the big pot. When the water in the pot boils, placing the dough on his left arm, he holds a thin yet sharp knife in his right hand to whittle the dough into the boiling pot, and lets the noodles boil in the water. Customers might often forget the taste of the noodles, yet remain deeply impressed by the acrobatics-like way of cooking.

Chinese people are very particular about food. The three essential factors by which Chinese cooking is judged are: color, aroma and taste. The Quanjude Restaurant is the most popular of the Peking Roast Duck restaurants. It uses an open oven, with fires from burning the wood of fruit trees. After roasting, the ducks become plump and claret colored, with a shiny gloss. The ducks are tender inside, with a crispy skin. They are usually served with thin pancakes, spring onions and a sweet sauce, so the taste is pleasantly strong.

The real charm of Chinese food comes from its taste, which lies in proper seasoning. The original tastes of the food, the post-cooking tastes, plus the tastes of other ingredients, all integrate together. This kind of aesthetic pursuit can obviously overwhelm more rational ones.

Cooking wine

chicken essence

salt

vinegar

soy sauce

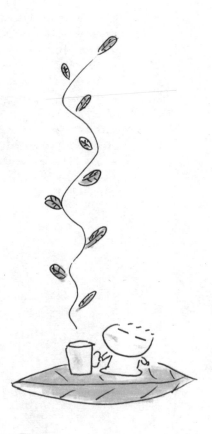

Tea Culture

Tea is the bud-leaves of the tea tree, an evergreen perennial woody plant. China is the original tea-growing region, and the first country to produce and drink tea.

Tea is a daily necessity for the Chinese people. As the saying goes: "The seven necessities are fuel, rice, oil, salt, sauce, vinegar and tea." Tea also has an indissoluble bond with art. Most ancient Chinese scholars enjoyed drinking tea, and entertained friends with tea, discussing arts while drinking tea, and pursued spiritual purity and tranquility by tasting tea.

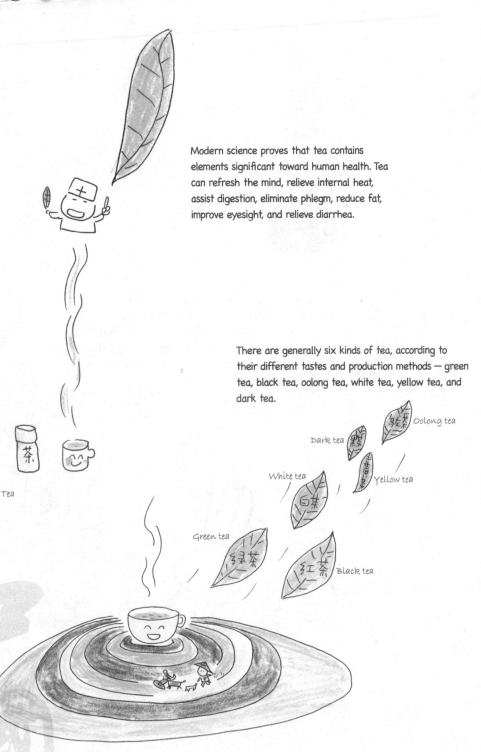

Modern science proves that tea contains elements significant toward human health. Tea can refresh the mind, relieve internal heat, assist digestion, eliminate phlegm, reduce fat, improve eyesight, and relieve diarrhea.

There are generally six kinds of tea, according to their different tastes and production methods — green tea, black tea, oolong tea, white tea, yellow tea, and dark tea.

Tea

Oolong tea

Dark tea

White tea

Yellow tea

Green tea

Black tea

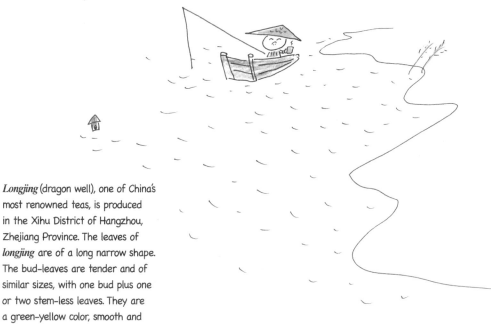

Longjing (dragon well), one of China's most renowned teas, is produced in the Xihu District of Hangzhou, Zhejiang Province. The leaves of *longjing* are of a long narrow shape. The bud-leaves are tender and of similar sizes, with one bud plus one or two stem-less leaves. They are a green-yellow color, smooth and faintly scented.

Biluochun, produced in Dongshan Town of Suzhou, is another kind of excellent green tea. *Biluochun* is famed for its early picking and refined processing. The leaves are slim, curled like snails; they are tender and of uniform sizes. The bright green leaves are covered with fine hair, and are picked in the early spring around the Qingming Festival. That is why the tea is named bi(green)-luo(snail)-chun(spring).

上碧螺春!!
Biluochun tea, please!

Here it comes!
来咯

The best tea ware is *Zisha* (purple clay) teapots produced
in Yixing City, Jiangsu Province. The clay for making
Zisha pottery is rich in iron with highly suitable mineral
composition, malleable for making pottery without
adding other materials. *Zisha* teapots have very good
permeability, to retain the tea color, aroma and taste for
longer. It also will not break or crack, even if put into cold
water immediately after boiling water.

100

Drinking Culture

An alcohol drinking culture is prevalent in China. People not only enjoy it, but on many occasions it is a cultural symbol representing rules of etiquette, as well as an atmosphere and a state of mind. Wine and poetry are indispensable. Drinking spirits also embodies a kind of life attitude and taste.

Liquor is among the most popular drinks in China, because people like the mellow fragrant taste. Maotai and Wuliangye are the two most popular brands across the country.

Traditional Festivals

China's major traditional festivals include the Spring Festival, Lantern Festival, Qingming (Pure Brightness) Festival, Dragon Boat Festival, and Mid-Autumn Festival. The national minorities have also retained their own traditional festivals, including Ramadan of the Hui people, Kurban of the Uygurs, the Water Sprinkling Festival of the Dai, the Mongolian Nadam Fair, and the Tibetan New Year and Ongkor (Hoping for Good Harvest) Festival.

Spring Festival. In old times when the lunar calendar was used, the Spring Festival, as the 1st day of the 1st lunar month, marked the beginning of a new year. After the Gregorian calendar is adopted Spring Festival generally falls between the last 10 days of January and mid-February. The eve of Spring Festival is an important time for family reunion, when many people stay up all night to "see out the old year." During Spring Festival, various traditional activities are enjoyed, notably lion dances, dragon lantern dances, land-boat rowing and stilt-walking.

Happy Spring Festival

Jiaozi (dumplings) are supposed to be eaten during the Spring Festival to bid farewell to the old and usher in the new. They are made of a meat and vegetable filling inside dumpling wrappers. The shape resembles ancient gold and silver ingots. *Jiaozi* can be served after 10 minutes of cooking in boiling water.

103

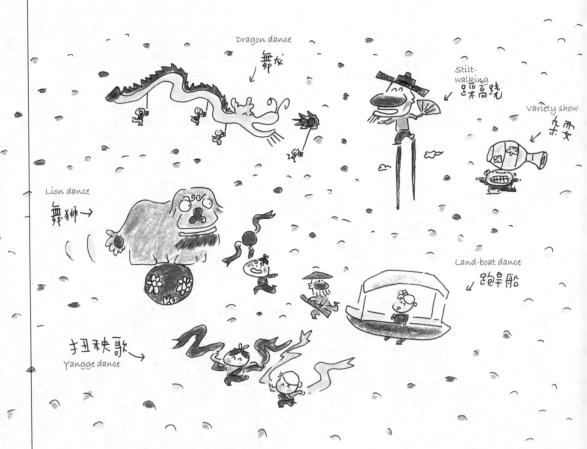

Dragon dance
舞龙

Stilt-walking
踩高跷

Variety show
杂耍

Lion dance
舞狮→

Land-boat dance
跑旱船

扭秧歌→
Yangge dance

看

During the Spring Festival, temple fairs are held in many places. The people of ancient China often gathered around the temples and held ceremonial offerings or entertainment and market activities. Nowadays, temple fairs are places where people amuse themselves and go shopping during festivals. Temple fairs are always bustling, with a variety of local snack foods and fancy folk toys sold, as well as all sorts of fascinating performances by folk artisans.

Lantern Festival. The Lantern Festival falls on the 15th day of the 1st lunar month, the first full-moon night after the Spring Festival. Traditionally, people eat *yuanxiao* and admire lanterns. The *yuanxiao*, round balls of glutinous rice flour with sweet filling, symbolize reunion. The tradition of admiring lanterns emerged in 1st century AD, and is still popular across the country.

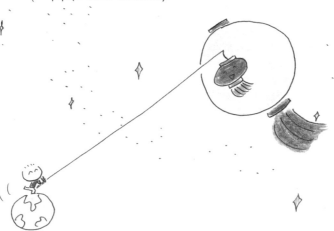

Pure Brightness Festival. The Qingming (Pure Brightness) Festival falls around April 5 every year. Traditionally, this is an occasion for people to make ceremonial offerings to their ancestors and clean family graves. It is also the time to pay respects to revolutionary martyrs. At this time of the year, the weather begins to turn warm, vegetation is bursting into new life and people love to go on outings, fly kites and enjoy the beauty of spring. That is why the festival is also called "Spring Outing Day."

—Family ancestors

Dragon Boat Festival. This festival falls on the 5th day of the 5th lunar month. Legend has it that this festival is celebrated to honor the patriotic poet Qu Yuan (c. 340–278 BC) of the State of Chu during the Warring States Period. As an official who failed to realize his political ideals and hold back his state's decline, Qu Yuan drowned himself in despair in the Miluo River, on the 5th day of the 5th lunar month. Every year thereafter, on this day people would take boats on rivers and throw bamboo tubes filled with rice into the water. Today, the memory of Qu Yuan lives on, as *zongzi* (pyramid-shaped glutinous rice wrapped in bamboo or reed leaves) remains a traditional food, and dragon-boat races are held.

Mid-Autumn Festival. The Mid-Autumn Festival falls on the 15th day of the 8th lunar month, right in the middle of autumn. In ancient times, people would offer pastries, or "moon-cakes" as sacrifices to the moon goddess on this day. After the ceremony, families would sit together to share moon-cakes. The festival came to symbolize family reunion, as did the moon-cakes, and the custom has been passed down to today.

In China, there are many beautiful legends regarding the moon, the most popular being "Chang'e flying to the moon." According to ancient Chinese myths and legends, Chang'e was the wife of Hou Yi. She swallowed an elixir stolen from her husband and flew to the moon. When the moon is big and full, the shadow on the moon looks just like a lonely woman standing under a big tree.

Traditional Civilian Residences

People in Chinese cities now mainly live in multistory or high-rise buildings, but there also remain some traditional residential buildings. Because of the diverse ways of life and social customs of different places and peoples, residential housing across the country varies greatly.

Siheyuan. Beijing's *Siheyuan* (quadrangle) is the most common housing in northern China. It is a residential compound with four separate houses around a courtyard. The principal room is built on the south-north axis, while the two wing rooms are located on both sides of it. The family elders live in the principal room, and the wings are bedrooms for the younger generations. This kind of design not only conforms to the ritual of "elders and juniors each in their places," but is also conducive to maintaining the residence's tranquility and privacy.

108

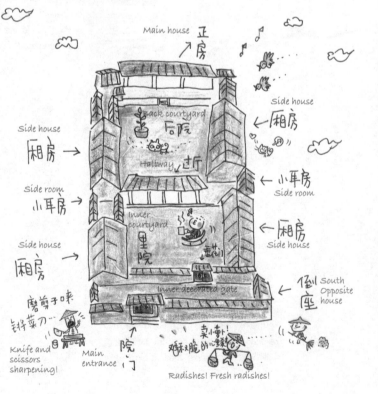

Main house 正房

Side house 厢房

Back courtyard 后院

Side house 厢房

Side room 小耳房

Hallway 过厅

Side house 厢房

Side room 小耳房

Inner courtyard 里院

Side house 厢房

Inner decorated gate 垂花门

South Opposite house 倒座

Knife and scissors sharpening! 磨剪子来 锵菜刀

Main entrance 院门

Radishes! Fresh radishes! 卖小事! 鸡酥又脆的心里美

Cave Dwellings in Shaanxi. The Loess Plateau in northwest China is famous for its natural conditions of dry weather, low rainfall and cold winters. The yellow loess earth, often as deep as 100 to 200 m and strong and impervious, provides sound material for cave dwellings. The cave dwellings are usually built on hillsides facing the south with exposure to the sun. Built in front of open ground, the houses are warm in the winter while cool in the summer, and very economical and comfortable.

红于夫的爱
妹妹你坐船头
哥哥我岸上走
恩恩爱爱
纤绳荡悠悠

How I wish to become your boat tracker! Let our love row us along the river …

Ancient Town of Zhouzhuang. In southern China, there are numerous rivers and tributaries, and people like to have their houses built along riversides. Zhouzhuang is reputed as a town of many well-preserved Ming and Qing buildings. The gray-tile-roof ancient residential houses tower on both sides of the narrow flagstone roads, facing each other against a background of rivers and stone bridges. Saturated with waterways, the scene resembles a Chinese ink-wash painting.

Tulou. In 2008, Fujian Province's *tulou* was included in the World Heritage List. In mountain areas, Fujian *tulou* are unique large-scale rammed earth residential dwellings, round or square, with circular *tulou* as the archetype. *Tulou* is a type of collective architecture in a grand form, embodying the local Hakka (or Kejia, 'guest') people's folk custom of living together in clans.

Yurts by the Tianshan Mountains. At the foot of the Tianshan Mountains in western China's Xinjiang Uygur Autonomous Region reside numerous national minorities, including the Uygur people. In the past, they lived as nomads and built felt tents as dwellings. The yurt has a wooden frame, covered with large pieces of felt. It is quite convenient to disassemble the yurt and carry it on horseback to new grazing lands.

看
中國

中國
功夫！

Chinese Gongfu!
(Kung fu)

Chinese Kung Fu

Martial arts or kung fu. Wushu, or martial arts, is also known as kung fu (literally, "skill"). Speaking of Chinese kung fu, westerners may immediately think of Bruce Lee. Bruce Lee was a superstar of kung fu films and founder of the Jeet Kune Do school. He acquired superb skills in boxing, swordsmanship and nuchaku weaponry, especially in three-section chain-sticks. He was the first to spread Chinese martial arts worldwide. He also greatly promoted the development of kung fu films.

In Chinese wushu circles, the Shaolin Temple has long enjoyed a great reputation, where shaolinquan has been practiced by monks for generations. The movement sets of shaolin boxing, totaling 72 sets, are all-embracing. All the movement sets attach great importance to basic skills. For instance, children's kung fu requires practitioners to receive very strict training from childhood, so as to master such complicated movements as "sleeping arhat" and "heel-up leg lift."

Taijiquan (or tai chi chuan, Chinese shadow-boxing), emphasizes body movements following mind movements, tempering robustness with gentleness and graceful postures. It is still a popular form of exercise today. Since it stresses the improvement of both skills and breathing, taijiquan can regulate the nervous and respiratory systems, to prevent and treat ill health.

A system of deep breathing exercises, *qigong* is a unique Chinese way of keeping fit. It aims at enhancing health, prolonging life, treating illness and improving physiological functions through focusing the mind and regulating breathing.

Generally speaking, all the above-mentioned schools of Chinese kung fu emphasize virtue and self-defense. Kung fu is practiced for good health and self-defense, rather than for aggression against others. This concept is very similar to that of traditional Chinese military thinking.

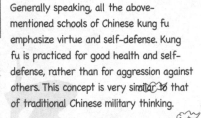

chinese
Kungfu !!

112

☆ 北京
Beijing

Beautiful China

When people visit China, most like to go see the Imperial Palace, Great Wall and Terracotta Warriors to appreciate the rich culture of this ancient country, while others like to visit remote areas such as legendary small towns in Yunnan to enjoy a laidback break away from the hustle and bustle of the world.

The Imperial Palace: Grand and Magnificent

Standing in the center of Beijing, the Imperial Palace represents the most superb ancient architecture of China as well as the largest-scale and best-preserved imperial palace in the world. Emperors of the Ming (1368–1644) and Qing (1616–1911) dynasties lived and ruled from here.

The Forbidden City has two parts: the front used to be the place where the emperor handled state affairs, while the back was the residence where the emperor and his imperial concubines lived. Major buildings stand in symmetry on the south-to-north axis line, displaying the grandness of the Imperial Palace.

Central Axis Line
中轴线

"家"
"Home"

皇上
办公区
Imperial Offices

Your Majesty looks really handsome in the robe!

Feeling fine ...
... 舒服 ...

皇上
这身衣服
穿在您身
真的是好
"靓丁子"

114

In terms of colors, every building has a roof covered by gold glazed tiles (gold, symbolizing imperial power, used to be a color that could only be used by the imperial court), walls painted a solid maroon red, and bases made of multilayer marble terraces. Against a gray background, these gorgeous red and yellow buildings resemble a heavenly palace, manifesting grand imperial power.

Come in, birdie!

Wood structures are one of the characteristics of ancient architecture in China. The wooden beams, pillars, doors and windows are often painted with vermillion, which symbolizes jubilation, and decorated with colorful designs like dragons, phoenixes, flowers and plants. The Hall of Supreme Harmony in the Forbidden City is the largest wooden hall in China.

The Great Wall: Praying for Peace

In 220 BC, the First Emperor of the Qin Dynasty (221-206 BC), who unified China, had some disconnected defense works, built earlier, linked up into a complete defense system to resist invasion from the north. This defense system, known as the Great Wall, was renovated in the Han (206 BC-220 AD) and Ming (1368-1644) dynasties, becoming the longest military installation in the world. The Great Wall winds along the vast lands of northern and central China, with most sections built with bricks and rocks on steep high mountains. The extant Great Wall is 6,700 km long, and not all sections are connected.

长城略图
Sketch Map of the Great Wall

Yumen Pass
玉门关

Jiayu Pass

Yanmen Pass
雁门关

Juyong Pass
居庸

Shanhai Pass
山联

Bohai Sea

Niangzi Pass
娘子关

Yellow Sea

Why did the Chinese people build the Great Wall? In ancient times, the south of China had developed advanced agriculture, whereas the north was still comparatively backward. Adverse natural conditions forced the northern nomads to migrate to wherever water and pastures were available, surviving on herding and hunting, and vying over the wealth of the farming people on the Central Plains to the south. The Great Wall thus became an effective military barrier against cavalries from the north.

There are some strongly fortified passes along the Great Wall, with the famous ones including Shanhai, Huangya and Juyong. Beacon towers make up one of the most important components of the Great Wall. These were facilities for transmitting military intelligence, using smoke in the daytime and fire at night.

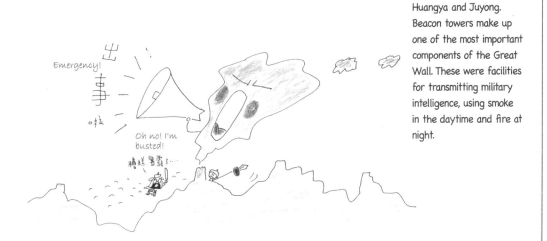

The core of the Great Wall culture is peace. The building of the Great Wall was closely connected with people's aspirations against war and demonstrated their incredible resolve. Today, the Great Wall no longer functions as a military fortification, but its unique architectural beauty is still amazing. The winding and zigzagging Badaling and Simatai sections of the Great Wall in the Beijing outskirts are two must-see tourist sites.

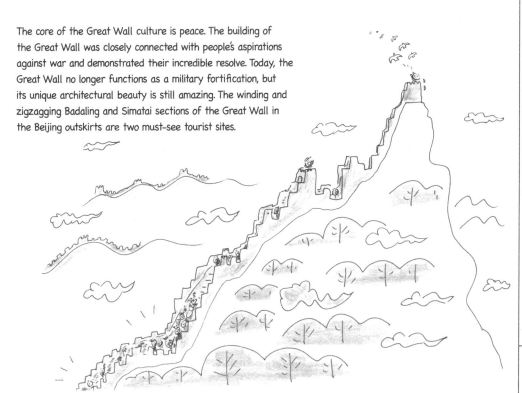

Imperial Tomb

The Imperial Tombs of the Ming and Qing Dynasties: Another World

Tombs may be called the palaces of feudal emperors in their life after death. The structure of these tombs is similar to that of palaces, with the front part comprised of ceremonial offering halls and underground coffin chambers at the rear. When an emperor entered the court, officials and officers would stand in two lines before the palace; so now in tomb areas, stone statues of officials, warriors, horses, camels and elephants are still found lining up in front of the tomb entrance.

morning sir!!

Qing Dynasty

Ming Dynasty

118

The Ming and Qing dynasties (1368-1911) witnessed a glorious period in the history of Chinese tombs.

The Ming Tombs is the general term for the imperial tombs of 13 Ming emperors, as the best-preserved tomb complex where the most number of emperors are buried. Covering an area of 40 sq km, the Ming Tombs are located by the Tianshou Mountains, at the foot of Mount Yanshan in Changping District, northwest of Beijing.

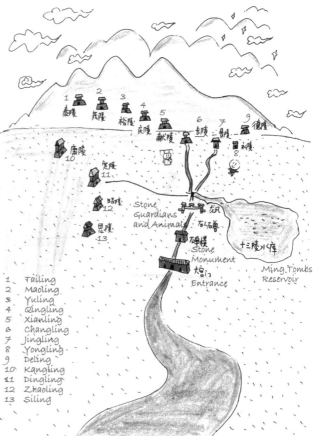

1. Tailing
2. Maoling
3. Yuling
4. Qingling
5. Xianling
6. Changling
7. Jingling
8. Yongling
9. Deling
10. Kangling
11. Dingling
12. Zhaoling
13. Siling

The Qing Dynasty (1616–1911) was the last feudal dynasty of China. The Qing imperial tombs can be classified into three areas based on building date and location: three early Qing tombs outside the Shanhai Pass, the Eastern Tombs and Western Tombs.

The Temple of Heaven: Where the Emperor Worshipped Heaven

The Temple of Heaven is a grand architectural complex of altars and temples where emperors offered ceremonial sacrifices to Heaven. The complex has a very neat and uniform layout, appearing grand yet simple. Built in the first half of the 15th century, it stands in the southeast part of the old city of Beijing.

As recorded in China's history books, offering sacrifices to Heaven was an official state occasion of great significance. Over 500 years, altogether 23 emperors, along with officials, officers and many others, held grand ceremonies to worship Heaven and pray for good harvests at the Temple of Heaven. According to established practice, the emperor came here twice a year to make offerings to Heaven for favorable weather and good harvests.

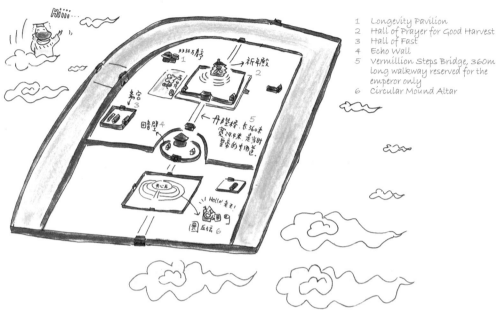

1   Longevity Pavilion
2   Hall of Prayer for Good Harvest
3   Hall of Fast
4   Echo Wall
5   Vermillion Steps Bridge, 360m long walkway reserved for the emperor only
6   Circular Mound Altar

Major buildings of the Temple of Heaven stand on a straight line from south to north. All the halls and altars face south and compose a circle, symbolizing Heaven. The function of the Hall of Prayer for Good Harvest is clearly indicated by its name. The Imperial Vault of Heaven holds the shrine for the tablet of the God of Heaven, while surrounding it is a round wall made of bricks — the famous Echo Wall. The Circular Mound Altar used to be the place where the emperor venerated Heaven on the winter solstice.

As the carrier of ancient Chinese traditions for worshipping Heaven, the Temple of Heaven has rich cultural connotations. Although these traditions are no longer practiced, the Temple of Heaven can still enable people to experience joy in nature.

I want to fly higher!

The Summer Palace: Museum of the Imperial Gardens

The Summer Palace is the world's largest and best-preserved imperial garden with richest cultural connotations. It is thus hailed as a museum of the imperial gardens. It used to act as the provisional imperial palace for short-term stays as well as an imperial garden. Built first in 1750, it was damaged in 1860 in wars and restored in 1886.

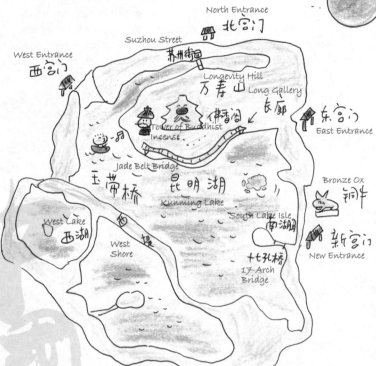

North Entrance
北宫门

Suzhou Street
苏州街

West Entrance
西宫门

Longevity Hill
万寿山
Long Gallery
长廊

East Entrance
东宫门

Tower of Buddhist Incense
佛香阁

Jade Belt Bridge
玉带桥

昆明湖
Kunming Lake

Bronze Ox
铜牛

South Lake Isle
南湖岛

New Entrance
新宫门

West Lake
西湖

West Shore

十七孔桥
17-Arch Bridge

Man-made landscapes, including pavilions, corridors, halls, temples and bridges, artistically blend in with natural hills and lakes. The most creative and unique is the 728 m paintings-lined Long Gallery, linking up other scenic sites and setting off the garden's overall beauty.

Covering a total area of 2.97 sq km, the Summer Palace is comprised of Longevity Hill and Kunming Lake, with the latter occupying about three quarters of the area. There are over 3,000 structures including pavilions, terraces, mansions, towers, corridors and halls, with the Tower of Buddhist Incense at the center.

Yuan Ming Yuan (or the Old Summer Palace), located near the Summer Palace, used to be the largest imperial garden in China and known as the "Garden of Gardens." It was destroyed by invading foreign troops during the Second Opium War.

Got here too late …

Confucius Temple, Kong Family Mansion and Confucius Forest

Qufu in Shandong Province is the birthplace of Confucius; the Confucius Temple, Kong Family Mansion and Confucius Forest were established there.

The Confucius Temple in Qufu was the place where emperors of each dynasty made ceremonial offerings to Confucius, so it is the largest in scale and highly adorned in China. Built in 478 BC, it has nine rows of 466 rooms. As the major hall, the Hall of Great Achievement is 31.89 m high, with corridors of 28 supporting stone pillars with coiling dragon patterns, each pillar carved out of one stone.

The Kong Family Mansion belonged to the direct descendants of Confucius. It is comprised of residential houses and offices. The mansion holds many historical archives, cultural relics, costumes and housewares of previous dynasties, all being valuable artifacts.

Better ... to just live well.

Existence or extinction

Life or death

Tomb of Confucius, the Greatest Teacher of All Time

The Confucius Forest covers an area of 200 hectares, as a cemetery for Confucius and his descendants. The Tomb of Confucius has a 6m-high grave mound.

Pingyao

Pingyao: Wall Street of Ancient China

The Ancient Town of Pingyao was first built 2,700 years ago. As a well-preserved historic city, it is one of the prototypes of ancient Chinese towns, looking almost unchanged from what it was during the Ming and Qing dynasties (1368-1911).

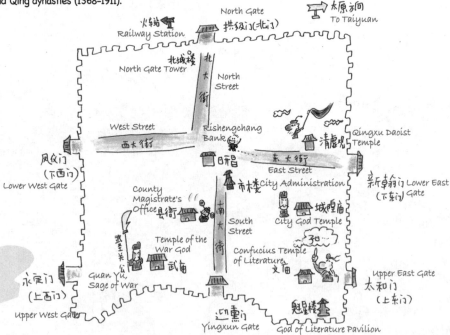

火车站
Railway Station

North Gate
拱极门(北门)

太原方向
To Taiyuan

北城楼
North Gate Tower

北大街
North Street

West Street
西大街

Rishengchang Bank
日升昌

清虚观
Qingxu Daoist Temple

东大街
East Street

凤仪门
(下西门)
Lower West Gate

市大楼
City Administration

新翰门 Lower East
(下东门) Gate

County Magistrate's Office 县衙

南大街
South Street

城隍庙
City God Temple

Temple of the War God
武庙

Confucius Temple of Literature
文庙

永定门
(上西门)
Upper West Gate

Guan Yu, Sage of War

Upper East Gate
太和门
(上东门)

魁星楼

迎熏门
Yingxun Gate

God of Literature Pavilion

The town now preserves six temple complexes and other old buildings like county offices and buildings. There are over 100 streets and lanes in their original form, while the shops along the streets remain mostly unchanged from when they were built in the 17th to 19th centuries. There are also over 400 traditional civilian residences retaining local characteristics.

看
中国

In the early 18th century, Shanxi merchants launched a financial revolution in China; for this reason, Pingyao is now hailed as the historical "Wall Street of China." Rishengchang Exchange Store, which enabled merchants to deposit money there and withdraw it from other places, appeared in Pingyao. This was the forefather of modern banks.

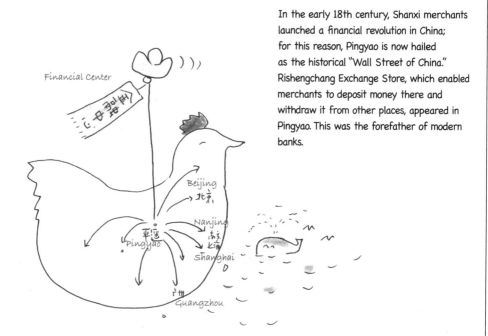

Financial Center

Beijing
北京

Nanjing
南京

Pingyao
平遥

Shanghai
上海

Guangzhou
广州

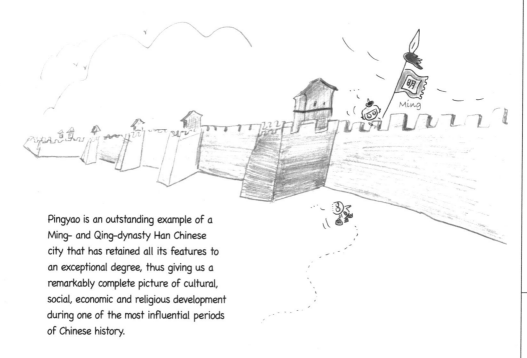

Ming
明

Pingyao is an outstanding example of a Ming- and Qing-dynasty Han Chinese city that has retained all its features to an exceptional degree, thus giving us a remarkably complete picture of cultural, social, economic and religious development during one of the most influential periods of Chinese history.

Imperial Summer Resort: Simple and Elegant Imperial Palace Gardens

Chengde's Imperial Summer Resort is 230 km away from Beijing. Its construction started in 1703 and took about 90 years to complete. Covering an area of 564 hectares, the resort is comprised of four zones: the Palace, the Lake, the Plains and the Mountain. It is the largest extant imperial palace resort in China.

Emperors of the Qing Dynasty built the Imperial Summer Resort with the political objective of appeasing and uniting national minorities in frontier areas of China and consolidating national unity. After it was built, every emperor of the Qing Dynasty spent a great deal of time there, handling major military and political affairs and meeting foreign envoys and national minority political or religious leaders from frontier areas.

Surrounding the resort are lamaseries, where nobility of national minorities from western and northern China came to pay respects to Buddha and the emperor. There are altogether 11 lamaseries just outside the resort.

128

First Qin Emperor's Mausoleum: the Silent Army

The Mausoleum of the First Qin Emperor is located in Xianyang, Shaanxi Province. According to historical records, the mausoleum was buried deep underground, consisting of palaces and posts for officials of all ranks and descriptions, collecting numerous pearls, jade and jewelry and other precious artifacts. But when the mausoleum was constructed, First Qin Emperor had the craftsmen lay many traps, so up to now the mausoleum has still not been fully excavated.

The mausoleum was built to imitate the layout of Xianyang, capital of the Qin Dynasty. In it were found the world-famous life-size ceramic figures in different postures, together with the war horses, chariots and weapons. The First Qin Emperor's Mausoleum has been named the "Eighth Wonder of the World."

First Emperor Qin's Mausoleum

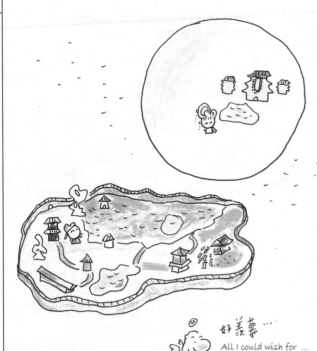

好羨慕…
All I could wish for …

Classical Gardens of Suzhou: Subtle Beauty

Feudal emperors of previous dynasties in China liked to build large imperial gardens. But most private gardens in areas south of the lower Yangtze River were secondary to residences, with each garden only covering a small area; in the limited spaces, natural landscapes were recreated in miniature, utilizing spatial changes, imitation mountains and rivers, as well as exquisite buildings.

Suzhou is a famed historic and cultural city in China, boasting nearly 200 classical gardens. Built in the 16th century, the Humble Administrator's Garden is a famous private garden. There are over 30 structures, such as towers, pavilions and halls, distributed around pools or on hills, making up different scenic sites. Along with the Lingering Garden, Master-of-Nets Garden and other classical gardens in Suzhou, it is on the UNESCO Cultural Heritage List.

The elegant classical gardens of Suzhou reflect the reserved character and unique aesthetics of the Chinese people. The design of these gardens seeks to recreate natural landscapes in manmade gardens. The layout is changeable and subtle. For example, there are few straight paths, as "winding paths lead to secluded spots"; flowers and trees are at different heights, and flowers blossom in different seasons ....

Mount Lushan: Perilous Peaks with Beauty in Infinite Variety

Mount Lushan stands in northern
Jiangxi Province, south of the Yangtze
River and west of China's largest
freshwater lake, Poyang. It rises 1,474
m above sea level.

Mount Lushan is one of the best summer resorts
in China. Its sea of clouds, waterfalls and
grotesque rocks are widely admired around the
world. Situated by water, Mount Lushan has a
rainy and humid climate, which endows it with
rich water resources, including 22 waterfalls, 18
sets of rapids, and 14 lakes and ponds. Moreover,
it is one of the nine best places for watching
sunrise in China.

From the perspective of history and culture, Mount Lushan is also famous. The Buddhist and Daoist temples and White Deer Cave Academy, which represents the Confucian school of idealist philosophy of the Song and Ming dynasties, blend in with the superb natural beauty.

Mount Tai, the loftiest of the "Five Great Mountains"

最为庄严的"五岳之首"
泰山…

welcome to huangshan !!

最险峻的…
华山

Mount Huashan, the most perilous peaks

Wudang Mountains: Holy Land of Daoism

Also called Mount Taihe, Wudang Mountains
are located in Danjiangkou, Hubei Province.
The highest Heaven's Pillar Peak soars 1,612 m
above sea level.

Since the Tang Dynasty (618–
907), Wudang has become the
sacred land of Daoism. Starting
from 1412, emperors of the
Ming Dynasty constructed here
a Daoist architectural complex
of 1.6 million sq m, the best in
China.

Wudang is also famous for its martial arts.
As one of the important schools of Chinese
gongfu, Wudang martial arts cover *Taijiquan*
(Tai Chi Chuan), *Xingyiquan* (shadow boxing
imitating the movements of animals or birds
of various kinds), *Baguazhang* (eight-trigram
boxing, shadow boxing characterized by
varied fist techniques and agile movement of
feet and legs, combining soft and hard boxing
tactics), Wudang *Qigong*, Wudang Sword, and
other boxing and weapon techniques.

I'm just a tourist!

134

Lijiang: Secluded Ancient Town

Built in the 13th century, the Ancient Town of Lijiang is located in Yunnan Province. It has no city wall, but smooth, clean and narrow flagstone paths, earth-and-wooden houses built solely by hand, and small bridges and flowing rivers.

Civilian residences in Lijiang integrate the essence of Han, Bai, Yi, Tibetan and Naxi buildings, and are vital for studying the history of Chinese architecture and the development of folk culture.

Can you guess the meanings of these words?

猜猜看
这些字的意
思是什么

A dream come true

A tree does not fall if its roots hold strong

A spring does not dry if its source runs deep

Having a baby

War

House

Sit and watch the clouds floating by

Travel along a river to its end

Lijiang is home to many ethnic groups. In addition to the Naxi people, who have a large population, there are the Han, Bai and Yi people. Dongba script is the ancient writing language of the Naxi, with a history of over 1,000 years. It is regarded as the only extant pictographic language in the world, a "living fossil" for studying the origin and evolution of human society and written languages.

Potala Palace: Heavenly Palace

When coming to Lhasa, Tibet, the first thing you see is the Potala Palace. It sits majestically on Red Hill under azure skies, looking resplendent and magnificent, with an air of religious mystery. In 1994, it was formally added to the UNESCO Cultural Heritage List.

The Potala Palace used to be the winter palace of the Dalai Lama. It is a large ancient palace complex at the highest elevation in the world. It is acclaimed as one of the top 10 wood-and-stone architectures in the world, highlighting the essence of Tibet's architectural, painting and religious arts.

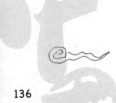

Mount Qomolangma: the World's Highest Peak

With an elevation of 8844.43 m, Mount Qomolangma (also known as Mt. Everest) is the highest peak of the Himalayas. It stands on the border between Tibet's Tingri County in China and Nepal. As the summit of the Himalayas, it is capped with eternal ice and snow.

I can see Mt. Everest.

我看到珠峰啦！！！

Mount Qomolangma is the highest peak in the world, and is regarded as the third among the five goddesses in Tibetan myths. Acclaimed as the "top of the world," it has becomes a "holy temple" in the eyes of mountaineers. Around it stand numerous peaks, with more than 40 over 7,000 m above sea level.

绒布寺

Rongbuk Monastery

珠峰大本营

Base Camp

The Rongbuk Monastery at the foot of Mount Qomolangma is a base camp for mountaineers. Built in 1899 at 5,400 m above sea level, the monastery is the highest temple in the world. The famous Rongbuk Glacier is not far away.

Shangri-la: a Beautiful Retreat

Many outside China get to know the mysterious name of "Shangri-la" from James Hilton's novel *Lost Horizon* which is popular around the world. But for Tibetans living on the Diqing Plateau in southwest China, "Shangri-la" is a name passed down by their ancestors. In the Tibetan language, it means "the sun and the moon in our hearts."

Diqing is one of the most mysterious places in China. There are countless ravines and canyons, snowcapped peaks, undulating grasslands and pastures. Tibetan, Naxi, Yi, Bai, Hui, Primi, Lisu and other peoples live a peaceful life on this beautiful haven.

Struck speechless by the beauty of nature ...

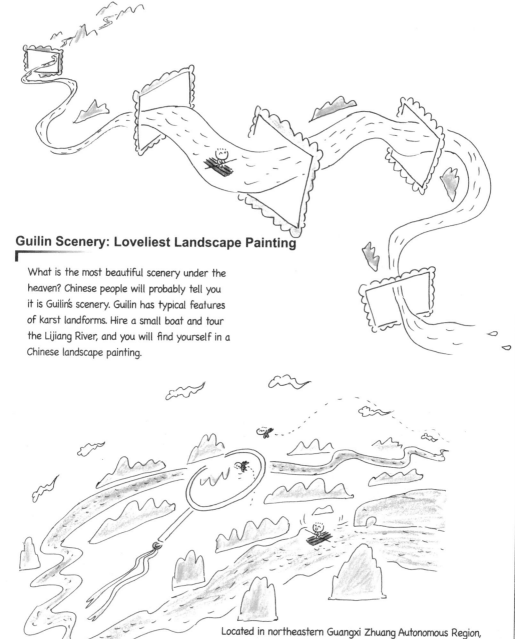

Guilin Scenery: Loveliest Landscape Painting

What is the most beautiful scenery under the heaven? Chinese people will probably tell you it is Guilin's scenery. Guilin has typical features of karst landforms. Hire a small boat and tour the Lijiang River, and you will find yourself in a Chinese landscape painting.

Located in northeastern Guangxi Zhuang Autonomous Region, Guilin is famous around the world for its beautiful mountains, clear waters, as well as fantastic rock formations and caves. The Lijiang River originates in the Mao'er Mountains to Guilin's northeast, and is 437 km long. It flows through Guilin and Yangshuo, resembling a jade belt winding through fantastic hills and beautiful mountains.

Yangshuo is an ancient town with a history of over 1,400 years. It has an old street of the same age – West Street, which runs along the Lijiang River. The street is paved in marble, with small wooden houses of blue bricks and cornices in graceful disarray.

Apart from Guilin, there are many beautiful landscapes in China ....

台灣的 明潭
The Sun Moon Lake in Taiwan

新疆的天池
Heaven Lake in the Tianshan Mountains in Xinjiang

有中国的夏威夷"之称的
海南岛
Hainan Island, the "Hawaii of China"

东方明珠
一香港
Hong Kong, the "Pearl of the East"

140

看
中
國

Opening to the World

04

When speaking of China, people tend to be astonished by its fast-growing economy alongside a flourishing ancient civilization. Today, China has become one of the countries in the world with the greatest economic potential. Its vast booming markets have attracted many foreign businesspeople, vying to invest in China.

China's Economy Setting World Records

Since reform and opening-up after 1978, China has achieved
rapid economic growth, breaking many economic records.

The rate at which China's economy grows is astounding. During
the 30 years from 1978 to 2008, China has maintained an
average annual growth rate of 9.4%. This reached 9.8% even
during the international financial crisis, with its Gross Domestic
Product (GDP) now ranking third in the world.

Opening to the World

China began implementing its policy of reform and opening-up at the end of 1978. Soon China established five Special Economic Zones (SEZ) in its coastal areas: Shenzhen, Zhuhai, Shantou, Xiamen, and Hainan. Subsequently, more cities and regions followed suit. These areas have been given preferential policies to help China's economy integrate with the rest of the world.

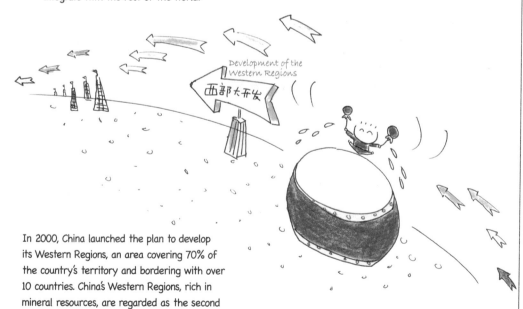

Development of the Western Regions

西部大开发

In 2000, China launched the plan to develop its Western Regions, an area covering 70% of the country's territory and bordering with over 10 countries. China's Western Regions, rich in mineral resources, are regarded as the second golden area for reform and opening-up, after the eastern coastal areas were opened years earlier. Now, the Western Regions have become a hotspot for foreign investment.

After the launch of the development plan of its Western
Regions, China put forward a number of plans to invigorate
its central and northeastern areas, thus promoting their
opening and economies.

So far, China is trading with over 230 countries and
regions. In terms of trade volume, its 10 top trading
partners are the EU, the US, Japan, ASEAN, Hong Kong,
Republic of Korea, Taiwan, India, Australia, and Russia.

China is becoming a new giant investor. A number of large enterprises have become competitive multinationals.

After 15 years of efforts, in 2001 China was admitted as a member of the World Trade Organization (WTO). Since then, China has further integrated with the world. In 2008 China's economy contributed to over 20% of world economic growth.

Nowadays, products labeled "Made-in-China" are found everywhere. World-renowned retailers, such as Wal-Mart, Carrefour and Metro, have increased their purchase in China in recent years. Chinese commodities are finding their way into the department stores and other high-end stores in many countries.

Emerging Alluring Cities

China's cities have witnessed the growth of its economy.
Especially large cities, such as Beijing, Shanghai,
Shenzhen and Guangzhou, are taking the lead in the
country's economic growth.

Beijing, a modern international metropolis, ranks fifth globally as the site of 21
headquarters of the world's top 500 enterprises. Its Financial Street and the Central
Business District (CBD) are signs of the capital's opening-up and economic strength.
In addition, the National Center for the Performing Arts, Beijing Capital International
Airport's Terminal 3, and the Olympic Bird's Nest have become the newest city landmarks.

International mainstream media describe Shanghai as a world model in terms of rapid economic growth. Shanghai, as China's biggest city, is also its largest economic center and international trading port. Its landmark buildings, including the Oriental Pearl TV Tower, Jinmao Tower and Shanghai World Financial Center, form the most splendid skyline of the world. The theme of the 2010 Shanghai World Expo is "Better City, Better Life."

Shenzhen, the earliest city in China's opening-up process, is one of the country's Special Economic Zones. Over the past 30-odd years, Shenzhen has developed from a fishing village to a modern metropolis, creating miraculous achievements in urbanization, industrialization and modernization. Shenzhen is presently developing itself into an ecological garden city.

Three decades later

30%...

It is predicted that in the 21st century, China will see the formation of 10 clusters of large cities — regions with the greatest potential for development. It is estimated that by the mid-21st century, China's urbanization would reach 65%.

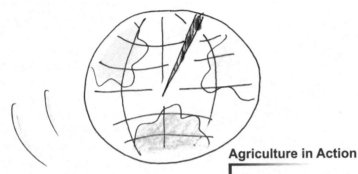

Agriculture in Action

Among the 1.3 billion people in China, more than 900 million are farmers. China has been a success in feeding one fifth of the global population with only 7% of its farmland. Now, China produces the world's largest amount of grain, cotton, oil plants, fruits, meat, poultry, eggs, aquatic products, and vegetables.

Now, China's agriculture is gradually striving towards modernization. Agricultural production relies more and more on high technology. In many agricultural production bases, computerized management has been achieved in the entire process from production to sales, although in some areas the primitive way of agricultural production is still maintained.

Yuan Longping, the Chinese scientist known as the "father of hybrid rice", has changed the history of rice cultivation in China for the latter part of the 20th century with his breakthrough achievement in hybrid rice. He is now working hard to popularize the "super hybrid rice," which can produce 12,000 kg rice per hectare.

While carrying out agricultural production, farmers also make the most of natural conditions by building eco-gardens and opening recreational facilities for tourists. These gardens enable tourists to enjoy beautiful scenery and experience leisurely countryside living by hunting, fishing and fruit-picking.

Strong Industrial Nation

Since the start of reform and opening-up in 1979, China has maintained high growth rate in industry. Since 1996, output of steel, coal, cement, fertilizer, and TV sets in China has topped the world.

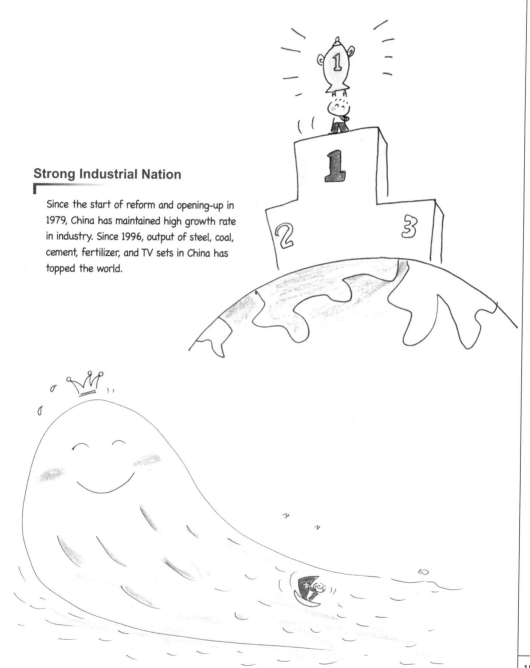

Saving energy, reducing emissions, protecting the environment and maintaining sustainable development are very important but difficult tasks. At present, energy consumption per GDP unit has declined markedly and sulfur-dioxide emission levels are being controlled, while water resources in some polluted river valleys have improved.

China ranks among the world's most-advanced countries in terms of satellite recovery, one rocket launching several satellites, rocket technology, and launching, monitoring and control of satellites on static-orbit.

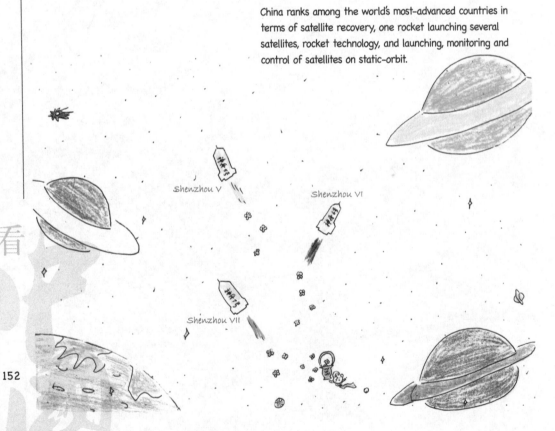

Shenzhou V

Shenzhou VI

Shenzhou VII

The IT (information technology) industry has become the first pillar in China's industry. In 2008, added value of China's IT industry ranked third in the world. China has become the biggest producer of monitors, cell phones and laptops.

China has participated in the construction of a number of optical cables overland and undersea, among which the longest Asia-Europe overland cable, 27,000 km, was initiated by China, running from Shanghai, to Frankfurt, Germany, via 20 countries.

The telephone has become prevalent in both urban and rural areas. China has established a mobile network covering almost the entire country. The country has also realized mobile roaming in over 200 countries and regions.

Convenient Transportation

Today in China the highly-developed railway and highway network makes it convenient for people to go anywhere they want.

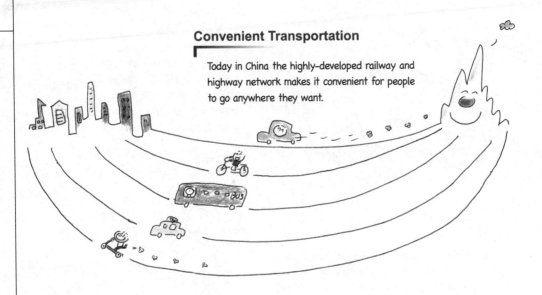

In urban areas using public transportation for inner-city trips is the first choice for most residents. Of course, some of them prefer taxis, which are faster than the public buses.

154

Most cars on the road in cities are private. Many families can afford to buy a car of their own, and more and more people will soon join them.

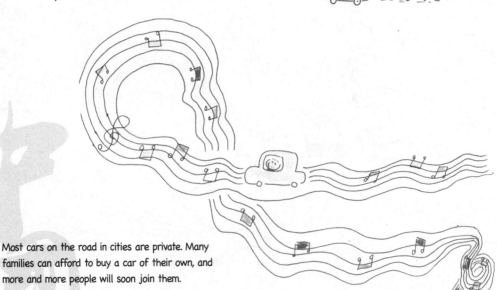

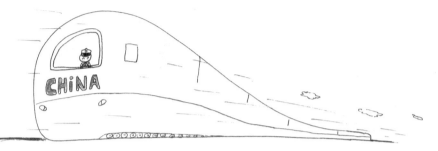

With only 6% of the world's total mileage, China's railways provide a quarter of the world's railway transport volume, ranking first in terms of train transportation. In cities express rail transit system is made up of light-rail, subways, suburban trains and other railways.

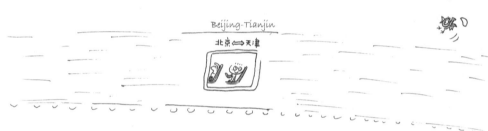

From 1997 to 2007 the highest speed per hour of trains in China has increased from 140 km to 250 km. On August 1, 2008, China's first high-speed railway, the Beijing-Tianjin intercity express, was successfully put into operation. This express railway possesses wholly self-owned intellectual property rights and self-innovation, reaching world advanced levels.

Conditions for passengers riding trains have improved. Many of the trains are equipped with air-conditioners and offer clean and comfortable riding experience.

The completion of the Qinghai-Tibet Railway is a great feat in the history of railway construction in China. Tibet is no longer a place difficult for people to go to.

China has 16 ports, each handling over 100 million tons of freight yearly. With regard to freights handled, Shanghai port has topped other ports of the world for three consecutive years.

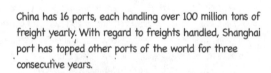

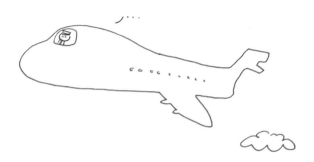

China has opened 1,506 air routes for civil aviation, of which 1,216 are domestic lines and 290 international lines. Most of China's civilian airlines are state-owned, or with the state controlling the majority of stocks. Private and Chinese-foreign joint airlines have developed rapidly in recent years.

本次航班飞往——北京！
Our flight is going to Beijing!

Taking a plane is the first choice for most ordinary Chinese when they go out on a long journey.

看

Sustainable and Steady Growth

To obtain the objective of economic growth
and at the same time protect the natural
resources and the environment on which
human beings rely for existence, this
sustainable development is one of China's
important goals during its economic growth.

拜托！留个活口吧！

Please! Let us live!

Stop!!
住手!!

Recycling Economy Promotion Law of
the People's Republic of China

The Recycling Economy Promotion Law of
the PRC took effect as of January 1, 2009.
This law goes beyond waste recycling, and
emphasizes high efficiency and economical
utilization of resources.

China is speeding up the exploration of
new types of energy — including wind
power, solar power, geothermal power,
tidal power and bio-power — in light
of actual conditions in different areas.

New Financial Trends

The renminbi is the official currency of China. The principle unit of renminbi is yuan, with jiao and fen as supplementary units. The Latinized symbol "¥," used before figures, denotes "yuan."

As China's economy strengthened, stocks and funds are gradually replacing bank savings as the major component of families' assets. Nowadays, bonds, real estate, insurance, futures, and art collecting have become popular choices in people's diversified investments.

Shanghai Composite Index   Timeline Graph for 09/09/2009
上证指数 [000001] 分时图 2009/9/9 — 14:59

2967.60
2055.23
2942.85
2930.48
2918.10
2905.73
2893.35
2767.421
2075.566
1383.711
641.855

09:30   10:30   11:30   14:00   15:00

The stock market is an important investment means for Chinese people. The Shanghai Stock Exchange and Shenzhen Stock Exchange are the two most important stock exchanges in China.

160

In recent years investment in real estate has become a hotspot for Chinese people. When people have more money to spare, the need for housing also inflated.

Buying insurance is also a way of investment for many Chinese. Now, China's insurance sector has become highly developed.

The Power of Brands

Thirty years of reform and opening-up have given rise to a large number of famous enterprises, which have created many renowned domestic or even international brands.

Lenovo is a global leading enterprise producing personal computers. When the enterprise was first created in 1984, it had an initial capital of only 200,000 yuan ($25,000). Lenovo has developed into China's largest IT company with advanced technology in personal computers.

Haier has 29 manufacturing bases worldwide. A total of 19 brands, covering refrigerators, air-conditioners, washing machines, TV sets, and water heaters, have been appraised as popular Chinese brands.

China Mobile has set up the largest operation network in the world, with the largest number of subscribers. Currently, China Mobile is the world's largest mobile-telecom operator in terms of market value. It has been included for the eighth consecutive year in the Fortune Global 500.

中国移动通信
CHINA MOBILE

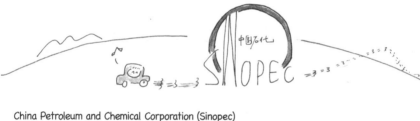

中国石化
SINOPEC

China Petroleum and Chemical Corporation (Sinopec) is one of the major petroleum companies in China, engaging in oil and gas exploration and trading, the production and selling of oil products and chemical products.

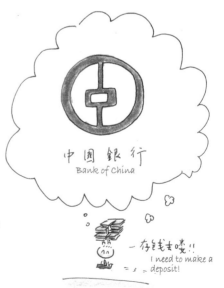

中 国 银 行
Bank of China

The Bank of China is a commercial bank with the state controlling the majority of the shares. Its range of business covers commerce, investment and insurance. The Bank of China was listed in the 10th place among the world's top 1,000 banks by the British journal *Banker* in 2008.

存钱去喽!!
I need to make a deposit!

Air China has a fleet of 256 planes, most of them Boeing and Airbus, operating 259 air routes covering 30 countries and regions.

People's Insurance Company of China (PICC), the largest insurer of non-life insurance in China's mainland, is rated upper-medium grade A1 by Moody's Corporation, an authoritative investment rating agency.

The State Grid of China is the largest public-service corporation in the world with construction and operation of electricity grids as its major business.

Tsingtao Beer, the oldest beer producer in China, exports the drink to more than 40 countries and regions.

Hengyuanxiang
Fashion Show

恒源祥时装发布会

After 80 years or so, Hengyuanxiang Group has developed into China's leading textile enterprise. Now it is the largest global producer of wool.

Bustling Commercial Streets

China has long bid farewell to an era of material
scarcity. Now, shopping is very convenient across the
country, with an abundance of products.

Zhongyang Dajie or Central Street in Harbin has a
1450-m-long pedestrian-only street, the longest in
the world.

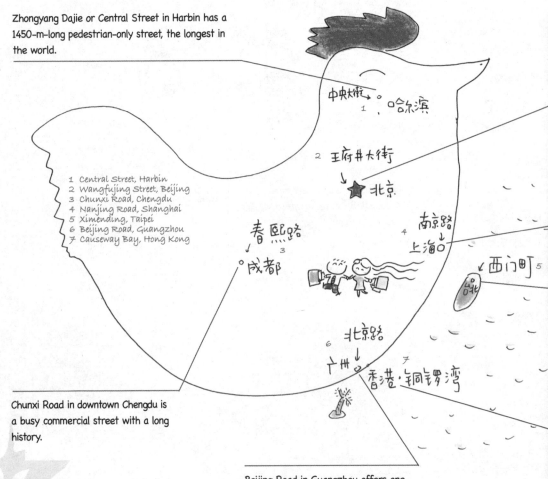

1 Central Street, Harbin
2 Wangfujing Street, Beijing
3 Chunxi Road, Chengdu
4 Nanjing Road, Shanghai
5 Ximending, Taipei
6 Beijing Road, Guangzhou
7 Causeway Bay, Hong Kong

Chunxi Road in downtown Chengdu is
a busy commercial street with a long
history.

Beijing Road in Guangzhou offers one
of the best shopping experiences in this
southern city.

Wangfujing Street has a history of more than 100 years. This one-km-long street lined with shops is known as "China's No. 1 street."

Nanjing Road is one of the earliest commercial streets in Shanghai, and also one of the most famous commercial streets in the world. Its total length is over 1,000 meters.

Ximending is the busiest shopping area in western Taipei.

Hong Kong's Causeway Bay, lying to the west of the northern shore of Hong Kong Island, is a central area for shopping, recreation and cuisine.

A Culture of Education and Science

05

During its 5,000-year history, China's development and progress has always been guided by education and science. Confucius, the great educator regarded through Chinese history as "Teacher of All Ages," has remained highly respected by later generations. China's ancient scientific achievements represented by the "Four Great Inventions" have also brought great benefits to world civilization.

China has the world's largest number of people receiving formal education. The popularity of education has stimulated scientific and technological advances, and over 60% of China's technologies have reached or approach international advanced levels. Some continuing innovations are remarkable, including: hybrid rice, the Qinghai-Tibet railway, launch of Shenzhou spacecraft, the Chang'e lunar orbit satellite, and so on. The Chinese have quickened their pace in exploring the unknown.

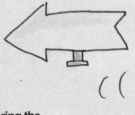

Chinese Ancient Education

China's ancient education included official education and private education.

Official education was conducted by either the central government or local governments. The highest ranks of official educational establishments were "Taixue" (Greatest Learning or Study) and "Guozijian" (Imperial Academy).

Ancient private education emerged during the Spring and Autumn Period, and the private school run by Confucius was the largest and had far-reaching influence. As the most famous educator in ancient China, Confucius had 3,000 disciples and 72 virtuous followers, nurturing a wide range of talent.

热烈欢迎 Welcome to our school!
报考我院…

書院
Private Academy

Shuyuan, or academies, were higher-education institutions that combined the collection of books, teaching and research; most were built with self-collected funds. Teaching took the form of self-learning as well as group-learning under teachers' guidance, but with the principal emphasis on self-learning.

In order to solidify their rule, ancient Chinese rulers established a system to select officials. The imperial examination system came into being during the reign of Emperor Suiyang (604-618). It aimed to select government officials through imperial exams covering a set curriculum. Candidates were recruited based on scores in different subjects. This imperial examination system lasted for more than 1,300 years in Chinese history.

"Super Man" National Contest

I'd like to thank the great Heavens, his Majesty, CCTV, and thanks to …

感谢老天
感谢皇上
感谢 CCTV
感谢…

状元就是你

You're the winner!

What a brilliant dream.

Modern Education

September 10th is Teacher's Day in China. This is a time when students give cards and flowers to teachers to express their gratitude.

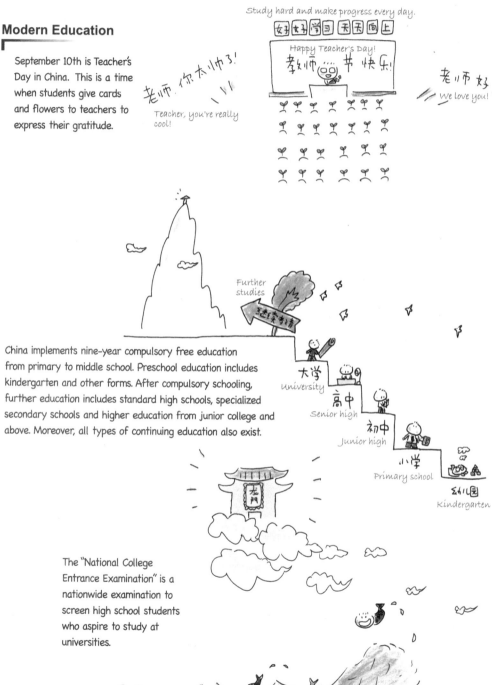

Study hard and make progress every day.

好好学习 天天向上

Happy Teacher's Day!

教师……节 快乐!

老师, 你太帅了!
Teacher, you're really cool!

老师 好!
We love you!

China implements nine-year compulsory free education from primary to middle school. Preschool education includes kindergarten and other forms. After compulsory schooling, further education includes standard high schools, specialized secondary schools and higher education from junior college and above. Moreover, all types of continuing education also exist.

Further studies

大学
University

高中
Senior high

初中
Junior high

小学
Primary school

幼儿园
Kindergarten

The "National College Entrance Examination" is a nationwide examination to screen high school students who aspire to study at universities.

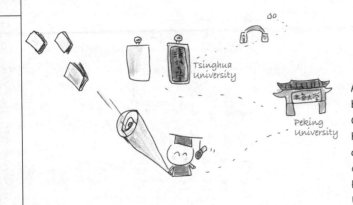

Tsinghua
University

Peking
University

At present, higher education has become gradually popularized in China. Generally speaking, China's higher-education institutions can be divided into regular universities and colleges for professional training. Peking University and Tsinghua University are best known in China.

In recent years people with university diplomas have kept increasing, particularly those with Master's degree or above. Continuing education is becoming the trend, as more and more people begin to take various after-work training courses.

172

To ensure that students from low-income families can receive further education, the government has initiated effective forms of assistance, including scholarships, work-study programs, subsidies for students with special economic difficulties, tuition reduction or exemption, and state loans.

New private schools have developed and prospered, satisfying people's different needs for education.

Ensuring Impoverished Students' Access to Education

"Project Hope" was initiated in 1989. Funding from the state and the general public has been used to construct primary schools or to improve educational conditions in poverty-stricken areas.

上学去喽……
I'm going to school!

From 2007 the central government has exempted tuition fees in rural areas for the nine years of compulsory education, with free textbooks also provided for rural students.

Modern distance-learning projects have been effectively implemented, with junior high schools in central and western rural areas equipped with computer rooms, as well as facilities for satellite-transmitted teaching programs and DVD equipment including complete teaching sets installed in rural primary schools. The Central Agricultural Broadcasting and TV School has grown into the world's largest distance education institute for rural areas, training farmers in practical technology.

All around the world
世界各国

中国 China

Foreign Students and "Chinese Fever"

China has engaged in active cooperation
and exchanges in education with the
rest of the world. No other country has
more people studying abroad than China.
Chinese students can be found all over
the world.

Every year over 100,000 foreign students
from 200 countries study or do academic
exchanges at nearly 600 Chinese
universities and research institutions.

Confucius Institute

Recently a wave of "Chinese Fever" has gripped many nations. There are over 40 million people all over the world learning Chinese today. China has established 256 Confucius Institutes and classrooms in 81 countries and regions, with the aim of teaching Chinese and spreading Chinese culture.

Ní Hǎo

Confucius Institute

Four Great Inventions

Gunpowder: The invention of gunpowder resulted from years of making pills to seek immortality or as medicine. In the Qin and Han dynasties (221 BC–AD 220), a Daoist alchemist who made such pills was inspired by occasional explosions. After numerous experiments, he discovered the formula for gunpowder: a combination of sulfur, niter and carbon.

Movable-type Printing: Before the invention of printing, cultural communication was conducted through hand copying of books. In the Northern Song Dynasty (960–1127), Bi Sheng invented movable-type printing based on block printing skills.

This is good paper!

Papermaking: By summarizing previous experience in making silk products, Cai Lun of the Eastern Han Dynasty (25-220) invented plant-fiber paper made from bark, torn fishnet, hemp, etc. This paper was good for writing. Before Cai Lun's invention people had to write on bamboo slips or silk.

Compass: The earliest compass was the *sinan* used during the Warring States Period (475-221 BC). The *sinan* was made of loadstone and resembled a ladle, and could either stay still on a flat square bronze plate or revolve freely. When still, its handle points toward the south.

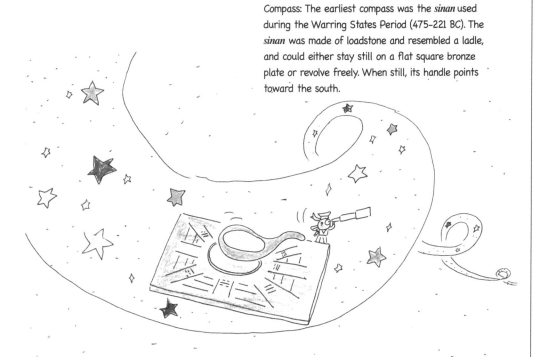

Ancient Architecture's Splendor

As an important component of China's ancient science and culture, Chinese architecture boasts a time-honored history and splendid achievements.

The square- and round-shaped shallow cave houses excavated at the Banpo Site in Shaanxi have a history of 6,000 to 7,000 years. Most were built with ceilings 50 cm to 80 cm under the loess ground, with inside stairs leading down from the door.

The Great Wall is a marvel in the history of architecture. Its unique construction structure, along with the complex and varied terrain it passes, makes it a true wonder in the history of ancient architecture.

Zhaozhou Bridge, built during the Sui Dynasty (581-618), is the world's oldest and best-preserved stone segmental arch bridge. The bridge has two small side arches on either side of the main arch. These side arches serve several functions: to allow more water to pass through, reducing the bridge's total weight and increasing its stability.

I designed it!

This bridge is great!

The Wooden Tower in Ying County, Shanxi Province, which stands 67.1 m high, was built in 1056. It is not only the highest and oldest wooden pavilion structure extant in China, it is the highest existing wooden structure in the world.

The buildings in the Imperial Palace, former home of the Ming and Qing emperors, are all wooden structures, with yellow glazed-tile roofs, marble terraces, and decoration of magnificent paintings. The Imperial Palace is rectangular in shape, enclosed by a 12 m-high and 3,400 m-long wall. Encircling the wall is a 52 m-wide moat.

Suzhou Classical Gardens are "forests within the city," naturally refreshing. The scenes in the gardens are varied: bridges across flowing rivers, blue tiles atop pink walls, winding paths leading to secluded spots ...

Mysteries of Traditional Chinese Medicine

Traditional Chinese Medicine (TCM) originated in primitive society. According to the theory of TCM, the human body is a unity of gas (*qi*), form (*xing*) and soul (*shen*). Through the four methods of diagnosis — observation (of the patient's complexion, expression, movements, tongue, etc), auscultation and olfaction, interrogation, and pulse feeling and palpation — and using treatment methods such as herbal medicine, acupuncture and moxibustion, Chinese massage, cupping, *qigong* and Chinese food therapy, TCM helps to balance yin and yang forces of the human body, therefore restoring the patient's health.

" Congratulations! You're in perfect health.

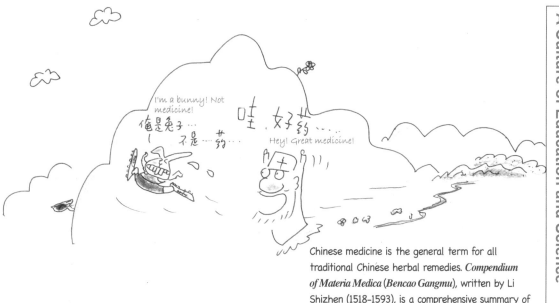

Chinese medicine is the general term for all traditional Chinese herbal remedies. *Compendium of Materia Medica* (*Bencao Gangmu*), written by Li Shizhen (1518-1593), is a comprehensive summary of traditional Chinese medicine before the 16th century, regarded as the "monumental work in Chinese medicine." There are as many as 8,000 types of traditional Chinese medicine, many of them are plants or animals.

Acupuncture and moxibustion are treatment techniques unique to China. Acupuncture is a technique of inserting fine filiform needles into specific points on the body and manipulating the needles to cure the disease. Moxibustion is a method of using burning moxa (prepared leaves) to warm up body regions and use the heat as a stimulant in treating various ailments.

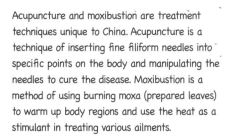

181

Rich Collection of Ceramics

Ceramics is the general term for pottery and porcelain. They are articles made from clay or clay mixture after being shaped and heated. Porcelain was not produced until the skills of pottery-making had greatly improved. Compared with pottery, porcelain requires higher temperatures, and sounds clearer when tapped. Regardless of its thickness, the surface of a porcelain product is translucent, and hard to scratch or flaw even with a knife.

Qinghua, or blue and white porcelain is famous among traditional Chinese ceramics. It features transparent water-like glaze, thin and light body, and blue patterns on its white surface. They were sold even as far as the Mediterranean regions by way of the Silk Road.

How a porcelain is made:

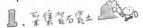

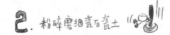

Jingdezhen is the "porcelain capital" of China, and even of the world. It has an over 1,000-year history of pottery production. The porcelain wares produced here are exquisite: "as white as jade, as bright as a mirror, as thin as paper, and as sweet-sounding as an ancient chime stone." Blue and white, blue and white with rice patterns, color porcelain and Famille Rose are the four famous types of traditional porcelain.

1. Collect porcelain stones and clay
2. Grind into a fine powder
3. Sift the fine powder
4. Form the main body
5. Paint on decorative designs
6. Apply an even layer of glaze
7. Heat in the kiln till hard

Hometown of Silk

Silk is exquisite fabric made of natural protein fiber obtained from silkworm cocoons. China was the first country to raise silkworms, reel silk from cocoons and make it into beautiful fabrics and products. Suzhou in Jiangsu Province and Hangzhou in Zhejiang Province have long been known as the "hometowns of silk."

Silk reeled from silkworm cocoons is a natural fiber which has irreplaceable qualities compared with other fibers and synthetics. Silk fabrics, after dyeing, are made into high-quality clothing, as well as decorative household articles, and other handicrafts, regarded as a "source of beauty" by foreign buyers.

During the Western Han Dynasty (206 BC–25 AD), the silk trade flourished and the trade routes became famous, known as the "Silk Road." This historic route started from Chang'an (today's Xi'an), out to Central and Western Asia, and eventually reached Europe, bringing silk and porcelain from China. In return, rare animals and birds, plants, leather products, medicine, spices and jewels were traded back to China.

Flying to the Heavens and the Moon

Feitian (flying apsara) is both an old and new concept for Chinese people. From ancient times, this was emblem of the Dunhuang Mogao Grottoes in Gansu Province and the symbol of the Dunhuang art. Today, feitian refers to the Shenzhou carrier rockets launched at the Jiuquan Satellite Launch Center in western China's Gansu Province.

The successful launch of the manned spaceflight Shenzhou V in October 2003 realized the long-cherished dreams of the Chinese nation to fly to the heavens. Astronaut Yang Liwei is hailed as the "China's first pilot to fly to the heavens."

Shenzhou VI, launched in October 2005, became China's second manned mission in space, which carried the two astronauts in orbit for 115.5 hours.

115.5 小时
115.5 hours

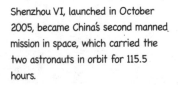

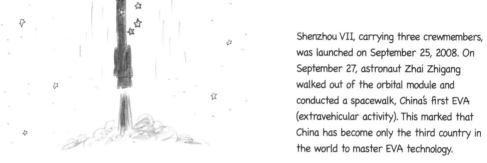

Shenzhou VII, carrying three crewmembers, was launched on September 25, 2008. On September 27, astronaut Zhai Zhigang walked out of the orbital module and conducted a spacewalk, China's first EVA (extravehicular activity). This marked that China has become only the third country in the world to master EVA technology.

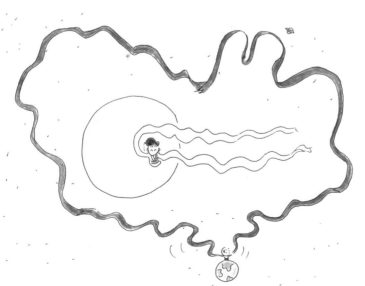

On October 24, 2007, China successfully launched Chang'e I, its first lunar-orbiting spacecraft, becoming the fifth country in the world to launch such a spacecraft. On March 1, 2009, Chang'e I did a controlled crash into the moon, a complete success of the first phase of the Chinese Lunar Exploration Program.

185

Railroad to Snow-covered Plateau

The Qinghai-Tibet Plateau, called the "third pole of the Earth," is renowned in the world for its high altitude, thin air, oxygen deficiency, and strong ultraviolet radiation. In addition, it is covered by snow all the year round and features extreme climate changes. The American train traveler Paul Theroux wrote in his book *Riding the Iron Rooster*: "The Kunlun Range is a guarantee that the railway will never get to Lhasa."

The Qinghai-Tibet railway was completed and opened to traffic in 2006. It is 1956 kilometers long, connecting Xining in Qinghai Province with Lhasa in the Tibetan Autonomous Region. As it extends across the highest plateau of the world, this railroad is also called Tianlu (Heavenly Road).

In order to protect the blue skies, clear waters and rare animals en route, environmental-protection investment in the Qinghai-Tibet railway alone adds up to over 2 billion yuan, 8% of the total investment of this railway project. The Qingshuihe Bridge in the Kekexili National Nature Reserve, for example, was specially built for the migration of wildlife such as Tibetan antelopes.

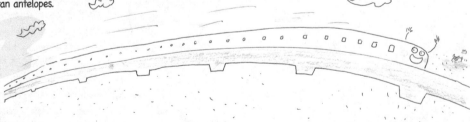

Three Gorges Dam Project — Rising above Smooth Rivers

The Yangtze River Water Control Project, or Three Gorges Dam, is located in the middle of Xiling Gorge — one of the three gorges (plus Qutang and Wu) of the river — known in the world as the biggest hydropower-complex project to date. The construction began in 1992 and was completed in 2009, lasting 17 years.

The huge Three Gorges Dam (TGD) reservoir, thus formed, can take much of the flood from the upper reaches, therefore greatly improving the flood-control capacity of the Jingjiang dykes in the middle reaches of the Yangtze. The TGD Hydropower Station is among the world's largest.

As the TGD reservoir began to store water, many landscapes formerly hidden in the mountains have been revealed, becoming new attractions in the Three Gorges area. Along with the formation of the 650-km-long reservoir came 37 gorges and sections suitable for white water rafting, 15 limestone caves, 11 lakes and 14 islands.

06

What's New and Cool

Thanks to China's rapid development in all aspects including the economy, culture and technology, in the 21st century the country has been exhibiting its great appeal in every aspect. China is like a kaleidescope of ever-changing styles, and the Chinese people's lives have thus become more diversified, especially experiencing the endless enjoyment brought to them by the digital technologies.

Clothes — Individuality and Fashion

Today, whether in such big cities as Beijing, Shanghai and Guangzhou, or in small towns, you can see people dressed in carefully chosen outfits in varied colors and novel styles. Everyone wears clothing that showcases their own individuality and fashion sense.

二十世纪七十年代······
The 1970s

二十一世纪······
The 21st century

All Chinese women have their own favorite styles of dressing, and can be "a girl of many faces," choosing different styles to wear for different occasions. Chinese men wear anything from suits to all kinds of casual menswear, or even trend-setting avant-garde clothes.

1 Only Beauty Dresses
2 Orient Beauty Vests
3 Playgirl Dresses
4 Maochang Garment
5 Pierre Cardin Men's Wear
6 Shanghai First Department Store
7 Nanjing Road Gentlemen's Wear
8 Shanghai Glamour
9 Hengheng Men's Wear

China's big market

中国大市场

Most world-famous brands are now available in China while local designer labels have gradually grown, especially labels featuring traditional Eastern elements, becoming distinctive in China's garment market.

Cashier

In China, people's clothing consumption can be divided into several levels. First of all, there are the high-end customers who pursue luxury brands. They always go shopping in high-class shopping centers. Then there are the majority of China's consumers who buy more common brands. Moreover, there are some people who buy clothes by looking for unique characteristics. Instead of labels, they care more about style or newest fashion trends. So they always go to various boutiques on street corners, and select clothing with strong individuality.

Dining in China

Dining is an important means of socializing for Chinese people. If you want to know what kinds of food the Chinese eat, well, put simply: "all delicious foods from around the world." Apart from the delicacies from various regions within China, you can also find all kinds of exotic specialties from foreign lands.

How do Chinese make dumplings?

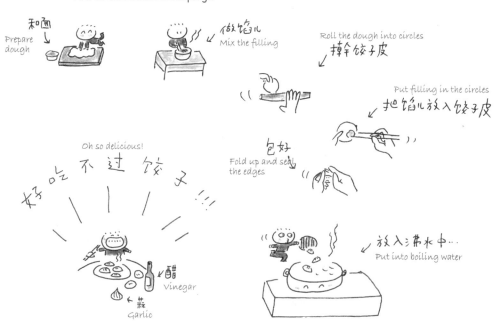

和面
Prepare dough

做馅儿
Mix the filling

Roll the dough into circles
擀饺子皮

Put filling in the circles
把馅儿放入饺子皮

Oh so delicious!
好吃不过饺子

包好
Fold up and seal the edges

放入沸水中…
Put into boiling water

醋
Vinegar

蒜
Garlic

In the past, the happiest thing for Chinese people during festivals was eating meat and fish, because back then meat, fish and eggs were all luxuries. Today, a healthy diet is what most Chinese people seek, and vegetables have become the new favorite on the dining table, with some people even preferring edible wild herbs.

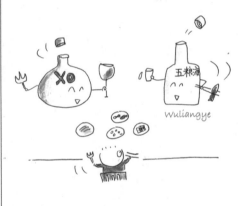

As for drinks, there are more and more choices. China is the motherland of alcoholic beverages. Drinking among adults has always been customary during festivals or reunions.

There are also many different kinds of soft drinks to choose from, both domestic and international brands.

Supermarkets are now the main source of food for Chinese people. For fresh vegetables, people still go to the fresh produce markets conveniently located in residential neighborhoods.

The different ways of cooking from region to region have resulted in varied styles of cuisines. The oft-mentioned "eight famous cuisines" in China refer to the following eight styles of cuisine: Shandong, Sichuan, Guangdong, Fujian, Jiangsu, Zhejiang, Hunan, and Anhui.

Wangfujing Snack Street

In Chinese cities, streets and lanes are filled with specialty restaurants serving food from other countries.

1 Wheaten Cake Boiled in Meat Broth
2 Stuffed Bun
3 Hand-pulled Noodles
4 Noodles with Soy Bean Paste
5 Deep-fried Sausage
6 Boiled Beef Stomach Slices
7 Mutton Shashlik
8 Rice Pilaf in Lotus Wrappers
9 Boiled Ram Head

Specialty snacks seem to be popular with everyone. Northern China is known for snacks made from wheat flour while snacks in the south are exquisite. The Wangfujing Snacks Street and the Donghuamen Night Market in Beijing which offer various specialties are always thronged by tourists.

About Housing

A story goes like this: two old ladies, one from China and one from the US, meet in heaven. The Chinese lady says that she had been saving up for her whole life and finally bought a house before she died. The American lady says that after paying back all her life she finally paid off the mortgage on the house she had bought 30 years ago. This story, pointing out the difference in consumer habits between the West and the East, has spread widely among Chinese people. In today's China, however, buying a house through mortgage has become most common.

The development of commercial housing has become more detail-oriented — green space, supporting facilities, cultural atmosphere and transportation — they are all important factors of consideration for choosing a house in China.

In the past housing was provided to people by their employers but now they have to buy a house on the market. Besides economically affordable government-subsidized housing, people who want to buy their own houses can apply for loans from the bank and take advantage of many policy preferences such as housing reserves.

In big cities, people who rent homes are increasing in number. Among renters, many are new university graduates, while others are taking up jobs temporarily in the city, including many foreigners now working in China.

For Rent

More and more urban families are moving to suburban villas, more easily accessible with private cars growing in number. The traditional courtyard dwellings in downtown Beijing have become especially expensive. These old courtyard dwellings are embodiment of the city's history and culture.

Network connectivity is good even up here!

网络正常......

Digital Life — "Caught" in "Networks"

China is striding into a digitalized information age; even the remotest town is connected to internet services.

"Network-dependent living" has long become the norm for many Chinese people today — their entertainment, communication, work and daily life are all heavily dependent on the internet.

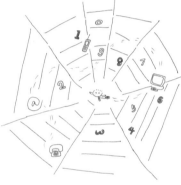

298 million! China has the world's largest number of netizens.

世界第一。

中国网民总数 2.98亿......

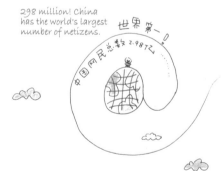

By the end of 2008, internet subscribers in China have hit 298 million, ranking first in the world.

In China's PC market, desktops have been gradually superseded by laptops.

The internet has become an important channel of communication for the Chinese people, with "net friends" a key part of one's real-life friends. Online chatting and email are widely used in various situations in people's life and work.

People can also get in touch via BBS (Bulletin Board Systems) and online communities. Through BBS, people are free to post and to reply. In cyberspace, perfect strangers, even from far corners, are thus able to chat merrily as if they were sitting face to face.

Blogging has also developed into a mature form of personal media in China. According to statistics, the total number of bloggers in China has now surpassed 100 million.

198

The internet has also enriched people's recreational activities, of which online games are typical, attracting large numbers of loyal fans. Online videos and music have also turned out to be a popular pastime.

Search engines have literally brought about a revolution in people's way of obtaining information. Wondering how to make Kung Pao Chicken? You don't need to go ask a chef of Sichuan cuisine — just search online. If you want to know more about China, why not search on Baidu or Google?

Want some new jewelry or electronics ...? You can buy anything via the internet. China's domestic website Taobao and international eBay are both online shoppers' favorites.

The internet has a vast supply of reading materials. If you want to read online, websites such as qidian.com and sina.com's book channel, are good reading sites. You can download the e-books that appeal to you, and copy them to a portable gadget like a mobile phone, MP4 or PSP, so as to read them anytime you want.

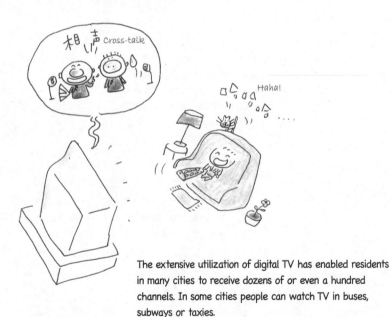

相声 Cross-talk

Haha! ....

The extensive utilization of digital TV has enabled residents in many cities to receive dozens of or even a hundred channels. In some cities people can watch TV in buses, subways or taxies.

看

Mobile phones have changed people's way of communicating. Their functions keep increasing, from making phone calls and sending and receiving text messages, to reading e-books, listening to music and playing electronic games, to accessing the internet, watching TV, and car navigation.

Digital cameras have also provided people with great convenience. Besides high pixels and memory, you can see the pictures as you snap away and choose those you like to have them developed in a photo studio. DV cameras are also changing Chinese people's lives, fully realizing anyone's excitement and dream of film-making.

Yinding Bridge

Leisure Time

In China people work five days a week. Major public holidays include the Spring Festival, Qingming (Tomb Sweeping) Day, Dragon Boat Festival, Mid-Autumn Festival, National Day and May 1st Labor Day. Employees are entitled to paid leave of various lengths.

Ah … people are so interesting …

人生百态……

I win!

俺糊啦!!

Checkmate!

将军!!!

…管上!! Ace!

This is a world of constant change … Obama's healthcare reforms, a typhoon hitting Taiwan, North Korea's nuclear tests, the H1N1 flu … Liu's son got into Peking University, I was given short weight when I bought the potatoes today …

国际风云变幻……奥巴马医疗改革 台湾风灾、朝鲜核试 和H1N1流感。 老刘的孩子考上北大了 今天买菜 缺斤少两三两

When getting together, Chinese people like to drink tea while playing cards or board games. Mahjong may well be called a quintessence of Chinese culture — people from everywhere love to play at their leisure.

马上要糊

Yep, I'm close to winning!

Shopping

As department stores and shopping malls are increasing in number all over China, shopping has become a regular pastime for many women.

Big cities have museums of different nature. Beijing has the greatest concentration of fine museums, which hold exhibitions on a regular basis. The Capital Museum was the first to introduce "Free Museum Days," and all that's needed is reserving in advance for free admission.

Holidays are generally peak time for travel. During holidays, tourist attractions in China are usually crowded with people.

People who have cars often go for outings to suburban scenic spots on weekends. Activities such as fruit-picking, fishing, barbecues and dining on local wild herbs are all very popular.

As for long-distance travel, options range from package tours to backpacking, driving to hiking tours. Chinese people like to visit other countries; Europe and Southeast Asia are popular destinations.

Backpack traveling is favored by young people in China. They decide the itinerary themselves. In this way they can gain a more thorough appreciation of local conditions and customs; it is more fun as well.

People who like adventures and challenges now opt to travel in their own car or by walking. Before setting out, they would prepare sufficient food and daily necessities, and normally sleep in their own tents at night during the trip.

Glamour of Entertainment in China

Both TV subscribers and TV sets in China account for one third of the total number around the globe, making China a major TV broadcasting power. China's CATV has become the world's largest TV network with the most subscribers.

In recent years, big-budget films have been especially popular with Chinese people. In 2008 *Kung Fu Panda*, a Hollywood movie, made several hundred million yuan in China. *If You Are the One*, a home-made 2009 "New Year movie," also brought in over 100 million yuan at the box office.

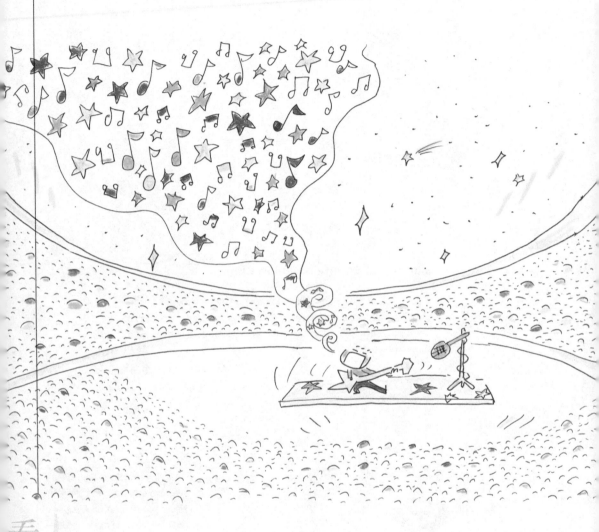

Pop music culture has greatly prospered in China.
Powerful star-creating forces have produced
successive pop stars whom fans go crazy about.

Ever since it was first introduced into China in the 1990s, Karaoke has been enjoying increasing popularity. At first, Chinese people sang Karaoke with simple home facilities; later as KTV clubs mushroomed, they became popular hangouts by young people.

As popular as KTV clubs are other nightspots, where different types of dance music are played — from slow elegant social waltzes to hot rhythms that appeal to youth.

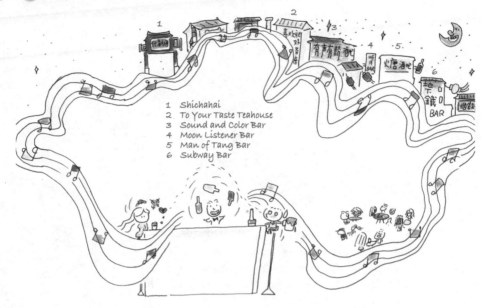

1 Shichahai
2 To Your Taste Teahouse
3 Sound and Color Bar
4 Moon Listener Bar
5 Man of Tang Bar
6 Subway Bar

Bar-going has also gradually become part of the stylish culture for the Chinese people. Bars have various styles — some are enveloped in a quiet yet enchanting nostalgic atmosphere, or have passionate yet unique bar singers; others provide bar-goers with facilities to sing and dance.

Flourishing pop culture has also given impetus to higher culture. From modern plays to operas, including traditional Chinese forms, to drumming, folk music and symphony, all are gaining popularity again with today's Chinese people. The newly completed National Center for the Performing Arts (nicknamed the "Egg") has become a special landmark representing China's modern architecture.

Surprise! A dark horse is born. The most astonishing upset in the history of the Olympics! Qi Qi beats Usain Bolt to become the new champion of the 200 m race!

Exercising for Health

Though busy and sometimes stressed out, people never ignore their health, but often actually care more about it. No matter how busy they are, they take time to relax as well as doing exercises.

More and more people work out in the gym. Yoga, Pilates, belly dancing and the like are especially popular with professional women; while jogging, swimming and bodybuilding are preferences of many men. As bowling, tennis and golf are becoming fashionable among ordinary people, the traditionally popular games like ping pong and badminton have much more followers.

Many Chinese people are fond of early morning exercise. In parks elderly people do fitness dances to music, or fluidly practice Taiji quan (Tai Chi Chuan), or just take walks while listening to music or the radio.

The 2008 Beijing Olympics helped spread the concept of "exercise" among the Chinese people. Starting from 2009, every August 8th will be "National Fitness Day" for people in China. Fitness equipment has been installed in many urban and rural neighborhoods.

Welcome   to   China!

Your friend Qi Qi.